Welcome

We are so glad that your family has chosen to worship with us for the last few weeks!

Highlands Kids ministry is all about partnering with parents to make a greater impact in the life of our kids. We strive to provide fun and age appropriate ways for them to learn to Love God, Serve people and participate in excellent worship.

9:30 service: Highlands Kids is available for kids birth thru pre-k. (no elementary class available at this time)

11:00 service has nursery thru 5th grade.

Please enjoy this devotional with your kids. It's a great way to learn together about the God who loves you!

If you have any questions about Highlands Kids please email children@thehighlandschurch.net

What people are saying about *Breakfast with Jesus*...

"Wow. *Breakfast with Jesus* is a phenomenal devotional to start with your kids every morning. This devotional dives deep into the study of Jesus' ministry and how we can learn from Him in our everyday walk. There is no better way to start your morning than with breakfast food and Jesus!"

-Ryan Frank, CEO/Publisher, KidzMatter

"So many of Jesus' most profound lessons were centered around a meal. Vanessa Myers has done a marvelous job following in the footsteps of the Great Teacher in her devotional *Breakfast with Jesus*. She helps children, and their grown-ups, explore stories of Jesus' life as they discover that God's great story isn't simply about 'things that happened long ago.' It's alive today...in each of us."

-Mark Burrows, Composer and Educator

"*Breakfast with Jesus* is a great way for children and their parents to start their day. Together they can explore a short scripture from the life of Jesus and see how it intersects with their lives. Author Vanessa Myers has created an age—appropriate way of reading and learning Scripture and then making it applicable to everyday life. Her 'Follow Me' activities give hands and feet to the Scripture and devotion. She has written a book for the way children learn and grow in faith."

-Rev. Debby Fox, Associate Director, Office of Congregational Excellence, North Georgia Conference of the United Methodist Church

"I like how Ms. Vanessa ties in a recipe with the book. I think that is really cool. I also really like what she says in her devotions. She did a very good job!"

-Violet Greene, 4th grader

"Breakfast with Jesus has been such a blessing! Vanessa writes with such enthusiasm and in a way that children can understand what God is saying to each of them, challenging kids each day to put what they learn into action. Reading *Breakfast with Jesus* has led to some very important conversations with my kids as they get to know how much Christ loves them and simply wants to be with them!"

-Katie Atcheson, Minister of Children and Families, Grayson UMC

"Reading these devotions helps me to think about Jesus each morning and reading it in the morning helps me to remember to show Jesus to others each day."

-Nolen Atcheson, age 9

"As a parent, I have searched for a devotional that is appropriate for my nine-year-old and also includes the rest of the family. *Breakfast with Jesus* exceeds my expectations! Vanessa Myers' manner of presenting the most important concepts of Christianity and learning to walk daily with Jesus is perfect for any age. I wanted this book for my daughter, but found myself more reflective and more aware of my life in Christ each time I read it. The 'Follow Me' feature that is included with each devotion encourages a family dynamic that is a fun and creative way to incorporate Jesus into our daily lives. The recipes are also a way to really find ourselves breaking bread with our Savior. I'm so excited to share this book with my family and friends!"

-Hollie Eudy, parent

Breakfast with Jesus

100 Devotions for Kids About the
Life of Jesus

Vanessa Myers

For the children at Dahlonega United Methodist Church.
You are a joy to teach and you bring a smile to my face.
I pray you will always remember to spend time with Jesus.

Contents

Acknowledgments. 11

Introduction. 13

1. The Word. 14

2. The Birth of John the Baptist Foretold 16

3. Favor with God 18

4. His Name Will Be 20

5. Mary's Song. 22

6. Jesus' Family Tree 24

Breakfast Casserole 26

7. Joseph's Dream. 28

8. My Son, the Savior. 30

9. The Prophecy Fulfilled 32

10. Joseph Obeys 34

11. No Room 36

12. The Birth of Jesus. 38

Bagel Dip. 40

13. The Shepherds and Angels 42

14. Hurry Up, Don't Delay 44

15. Simeon's Bucket List. 46

16. The Wise Men 48

17. Jesus as a Child. 50

18. Be a Witness 52

Monkey Bread 54

19. The Baptism of Jesus 56

20. Into the Wilderness. 58

21. Come, Follow Me. 60

22. Water into Wine 62

23. Born Again. 64

24. The Woman at the Well 66

Sausage Balls 68

25. The First Evangelist 70

26. Jesus Heals the Sick 72

27. Jesus Prays Alone 74

28. Because You Say So 76

29. The Beatitudes 78

30. Blessed Are the Poor in Spirit 80

Pumpkin Bread 82

31. Blessed Are Those Who Mourn 84

32. Blessed Are the Meek 86

33. Blessed Are the Hungry & Thirsty 88

34. Blessed Are the Merciful 90

35. Blessed Are the Pure in Heart 92

36. Blessed Are the Peacemakers 94

Ham Breakfast Rolls 96

37. Blessed Are Those Who Are Persecuted 98

38. Love Your Enemies 100

39. Jesus Teaches Prayer 102

40. Do Not Worry 104

41. The Golden Rule 106

42. Building on the Rock 108

Cream Cheese Banana Bread 110

43. Judging Others 112

44. Forgiveness 114

45. Give to Others 116

46. The Parable of the Sower 118

47. Be the Light 120

48. Jesus Calms the Storm 122

Cinnamon Toast 124

49. The Pool of Healing 126

50. The Workers Are Few 128

51. Jesus Feeds 5,000 People 130

52. Jesus Walks on Water 132

53. Bread of Life 134

54. Hard Teaching. 136

Butter Top Coffee Cake. 138

55. Dazzling White 140

56. Listen to Him. 142

57. Jesus the Good Shepherd 144

58. Parable of the Good Samaritan 146

59. Martha and Mary. 148

60. Parable of the Great Banquet 150

Fruit Salad. 152

61. Parable of the Lost Sheep. 154

62. Parable of the Lost Coin 156

63. Parable of the Lost Son 158

64. Jesus Heals Ten Men. 160

65. Jesus and the Children 162

66. The Rich Man and the Kingdom of God 164

Homemade Biscuits 166

67. Parable of the Workers in the Vineyard 168

68. Lazarus' Death 170

69. Jesus Wept. 172

70. Another Miracle. 174

71. Jesus Predicts His Death 176

72. A Mother's Request. 178

Strawberry Banana Smoothie 180

73. Blind Bartimaeus 182

74. Zacchaeus 184

75. The Triumphal Entry. 186

76. The Widow's Offering. 188

77. Jesus at the Temple. 190

78. Give to God 192

Breakfast Burrito. 194

79. On Whose Authority?. 196

80. He is Coming Again 198

81. The Anointing of Jesus 200

82. Judas Agrees to Betray Jesus. 202

83. The Last Supper 204

84. Garden of Gethsemane. 206

Homemade Waffles. 208

85. One Way 210

86. The Holy Spirit 212

87. Peace I Leave With You 214

88. Jesus is Arrested. 216

89. Peter Denies Jesus 218

90. Crucifixion of Jesus. 220

French Toast. 222

91. Jesus' Burial 224

92. He is Risen 226

93. Jesus Appears to Mary Magdalene. 228

94. The Road to Emmaus. 230

95. Jesus Appears to the Disciples 232

96. Doubting Thomas. 234

Spiced Tea. 236

97. Breakfast on the Beach 238

98. Peter, Do You Love Me?. 240

99. Jesus' Ascension. 242

100. Many More 244

About the Author 247

Acknowledgments

First, I want to thank God for giving me another idea for a book. This time it's for children and it comes out of my desire for them to walk closely with Jesus.

I also want to thank my friend, Shana Corbin, for asking me for recommendations for a children's devotional. Her question was God speaking to me and prompting me to write this devotional for children. And I thank Shana for her beautiful book cover design. She is so talented!

I am also very thankful for the children that I work with each week at Dahlonega UMC. They inspire me to continue teaching and sharing Jesus with them. I am blessed to be their leader at the church.

I am always grateful for my husband, Andrew, who supports me in my writing. And I am so thankful for my two daughters, Rae Lynn and Shelby. I am so proud of you and so blessed to be your mother. May you always remember that Jesus is with you and that He loves you.

Introduction

Did you know that Jesus invited His disciples to have breakfast with Him on the beach?

In John 21, we find the story of Jesus when He appears to the disciples on the shore of Galilee, after He's been resurrected. He shows them where to cast their net to catch fish. They caught a full net of fish (153 to be exact). As they approached the shore, they saw a charcoal fire burning with fish already on it, along with some bread. Then Jesus said to them, "Come and have breakfast." (John 21:12). And the disciples ate and talked with Jesus. One of the last things Jesus said to His disciples that morning was "Follow me." (John 21:19b).

As I read and reflect on this story, I find that Jesus was teaching them a few things. First, He wanted them to come eat and fellowship with Him. Second, He wanted them to spend time with Him in the early morning hours. And third, He wanted them to follow Him. I think it is so important that we start off our day with Jesus. This is not just for grown-ups, but for kids too. Jesus wants to hang out with you every day. And spending just 5-10 minutes with Him before you go to school will help start off your day well.

In this 100-day devotional, you will be hanging out with Jesus each morning and learning more about Him. Each devotion comes from one of the four Gospels (Matthew, Mark, Luke and John). As you read each devotion, pretend like you are one of the disciples and Jesus is teaching you…much like He did that morning on the beach with them. And make sure to grab some breakfast and eat with Jesus as you spend time with Him.

Each day's reading consists of the following things: Scripture verse, devotion, prayer, and a "Follow Me" idea (a way you can follow Jesus that day). You'll also find scattered throughout the book some breakfast recipes that you and your parents can make together.

My hope for this book is that you create a habit of spending time with Jesus each morning. Enjoy your breakfast with Jesus!

The Word
John 1:1–5

"In the beginning was the Word, and the Word was with God, and the Word was God." John 1:1

Make a list right now of words that describe Jesus. Ready, set, go!

_____

_____

_____

_____

I am sure you have some good ones listed. Maybe some you wrote were "love," "friend," "Savior," "forgiving," or "compassionate." But what about the word "word?" Did you have that one listed? I am thinking you probably did not write that one down. It's not one you immediately think of when you think about Jesus.

In the book of John, we discover that Jesus is the Word. To help us know what that means, I thought it would be good for us to write out John 1:1-3. Just fill in the blank. These verses are from the NIV Bible:

"In the beginning was the _____, and the Word was with _____, and the Word was _____. He was with God in the _____. Through him all _____ were _____; without him _____ was made that has been made."

From these verses, we can see that Jesus is the Word. He was with God in the beginning and He is God. Through Him all things were made. This name for Jesus shows us that He is the One who came to earth to reveal who God is and tell us what God is like. And He can do that because He is God and He was with God in the beginning.

Now you can add a new word for Jesus to your list. Go back up the page now and add "Word." And if someone asks you what it means you can now tell them!

Word of Life, we give thanks that You are God. We give thanks that You created everything in this world. We give thanks for revealing to us what God is like. We give thanks for You, Jesus. We praise You, Lord. Amen.

Follow Me

Plan to go on a hike with your family. On this hike, make a point to thank God for everything you see. Thanking God for things He created helps you to remember that He is our Creator.

The Birth of John the Baptist Foretold

Luke 1:5–25

"But the angel said to him: 'Do not be afraid, Zechariah; your prayer has been heard. Your wife Elizabeth will bear you a son, and you are to call him John.'" Luke 1:13

Have you ever prayed for something and didn't believe God heard you because it took a long time for God to answer it? Maybe you felt frustrated. Maybe you thought God didn't care or your request wasn't important enough. Maybe you felt like giving up.

I believe that's exactly how Zechariah felt.

Zechariah had a wife named Elizabeth. They were married, but Elizabeth was unable to have kids. Still, Zechariah prayed for them to be blessed with children. I like to believe that Zechariah felt much like we feel when our prayers go unanswered. How much longer should he pray for a child to be born to them? Maybe he was just about ready to give up, but then something amazing happened.

Zechariah was a priest. He was selected to go inside the innermost sanctuary of the temple to offer incense to God. While he was in there, an angel appeared to him and spoke the words he had been longing to hear: "Do not be afraid, Zechariah; your prayer has been heard. Your wife Elizabeth will bear a son, and you are to call him John." (Luke1:13).

He had to have been feeling several different emotions: shocked, scared, amazed, happy, joyful. So many different ways to react to the news of a child to be born. But then the angel goes on to say some other pretty shocking and amazing things about the child to be born to him: he will be great in the sight of the Lord, he will turn many people of Israel to God, he will help prepare people for the coming of Jesus Christ (Luke1:15-17). Not only would Zechariah be blessed with a child, but this child would help point others to Jesus.

There may be times in your life when you pray for a long time and don't get an answer from God. But my hope is that you won't give up praying. God hears your prayer. Just remember that God's time is different than our time. And remember that God may answer your prayer but in a different way than you thought…in a way that's better than what you could have ever imagined. Just as He did for Zechariah. Keep praying…God hears you.

Father God, thank You for always hearing my prayers. Help me to never give up and remind me that You are always with me. Amen.

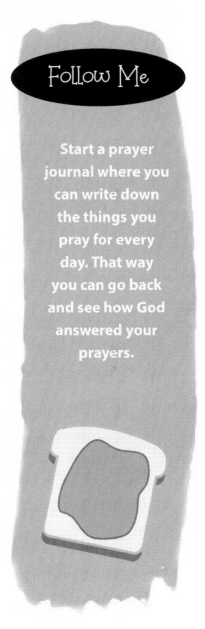

Follow Me

Start a prayer journal where you can write down the things you pray for every day. That way you can go back and see how God answered your prayers.

3

Favor with God
Luke 1:26-30

"But the angel said to her, 'Do not be afraid, Mary; you have found favor with God.'" Luke 1:30

Do you know what it feels like to be favored by someone? To be favored means you have the support or approval of someone. You may have been favored by your parents, your teacher, your coach, or your friends. It feels really good to know that you have the support of someone and that they like you!

Now take that feeling you have when you have been favored and multiply it by a trillion. That must have been how Mary felt when the angel Gabriel came to visit her and told her she was favored by God.

First of all, what a shock to have a visit from an angel! I can only imagine what she was feeling from that encounter. But what a double shock to hear the angel say this: "Greetings, you who are highly favored! The Lord is with you." (Luke 1:28). I would have probably reacted the same way Mary did. The NIV Bible says that Mary was "greatly troubled at his words" (Luke 1:29). Other translations say Mary was confused, perplexed, disturbed, and shaken. Hearing these words from one of God's angels would have left me in a state of confusion, too.

Gabriel noticed the expression on her face and came back with a calming response: "Do not be afraid, Mary; you have found favor with God." (Luke 1:30). But Gabriel has yet to tell her why she has found favor with God and what God will do with her. That doesn't come until the next verse, which we will look at tomorrow.

Mary had found favor with God. He had chosen her. And you know what…He has chosen you. God has called you to do great things for Him. No matter what God calls you to do, remember to listen and obey, just as Mary did.

Heavenly Father, thank You for showing favor to Mary. Help me to remember that You have favored me and chosen me to do great things for You. And help me to always listen to You. In Jesus' name, Amen.

Follow Me

Make birthday cards for children who are in foster care. Let them know that God favors them and He loves them.

To find out more information, visit the Foundation for Foster Children website: https://foundationforfosterchildren.org/. Click on the Get Involved link and then the Volunteer link. The instructions for birthday cards are listed there.

4

His Name Will Be

Luke 1:31-33

"You will conceive and give birth to a son, and you are to call him Jesus." Luke 1:31

I love to learn the meaning of a person's name. When I found out the meaning of my name, I thought it was very fitting. The name Vanessa means "butterfly" in Greek. And do you know the one thing I have loved since I was a kid…butterflies! What a cool name for me!

In the next few verses of Luke 1, we see the angel Gabriel delivering the news that Mary will become pregnant and will give birth to a Son. And then the angel said what she was to name the baby, "Jesus." Mary didn't have to toss around baby names for nine months. She didn't have to search through baby name books for that perfect name. She didn't have to Google "best baby names." She didn't even have to argue with Joseph about what they would name Him. She was given a name. And it was a perfect name. Do you know what Jesus means? It means "Savior." And that's exactly what Jesus is for us!

After the angel says she is to name Him Jesus, he tells her exactly who Jesus will be. He will be "the Son of the Most High. The Lord God will give him the throne of his father David." (Luke 1:32). He also throws in there that He will be the King of Israel and will reign forever.

We know from other Scriptures that Jesus will go on to have many names. I found an article online that listed fifty names for Jesus. Some of those names are: Prince of Peace, Mighty God, Holy

One, King of Kings, Wonderful Counselor, Emmanuel, Jehovah-Ji-reh, El Roi, Elohim, and so many more.

Each of these names brings us peace and hope. So next time you are scared or anxious or worried, remember that Jesus' name means Savior and He has come to give eternal life to all those who believe. Thank You, God, for sending Jesus, Your Son, to be our Savior!

Holy God, thank You for Jesus. Help me to remember His name and speak His name to everyone. In Jesus' name, Amen.

Follow Me

Make "Names of Jesus" cards to put around your house. Take the names listed above for Jesus (and any other ones that you and your parents can think of) and write the name on a card. Decorate the card and then each week post one of the cards on your fridge to remind your family of the many names of Jesus.

Mary's Song
Luke 1:39–56

"And Mary said: 'My soul glorifies the Lord and my spirit rejoices in God my Savior.'" Luke 1:46-47

What do you like to do when you are happy?

One of the things I love to do is sing and dance. My husband usually tells me I'm being too loud when I'm singing around the house. (Mostly because it always seems to be at a time when he's watching a football game.) I also really like to sing loud in the car when I am by myself. There's no one to tell me to stop singing! I love to sing, and I love to praise the Lord through worship songs.

I think I take after Mary when it comes to singing when I am happy. After Elizabeth (her cousin) cried out with joy and told her how blessed she was, Mary broke out into song. Her song is known as the Magnificat (I know…it's a big word). In this song she praises God for what He has done for her. Those praises include: letting it be known that the Lord is greater than anything else, glorifying His name and giving praise to Him, singing about the favor God has shown her. She recognizes how unlikely she is to be someone God would look upon and use for His glory. But then she quickly realizes that people will look at her and see how truly blessed she is.

There will be times in your life when you can't believe that God chose you to do something for Him. That could be something big like writing a book or starting a ministry for the poor, or it could be something as simple as talking with a friend about Jesus or even inviting someone to your house for a meal. No matter what God asks you to do, do it with joy. And hey…you can break into song like Mary if you like. You know I wouldn't mind, and I might even sing along with you. Be like Mary and praise God for choosing you to do His work on this earth.

Most Holy God, thank You for helping me to see the joy that Mary felt as she realized she would be the mother of the Son of God. Help me to be like Mary and always praise You. In Jesus' name, Amen.

Follow Me

If you love to sing, join the children's choir at your church. Or if your school does a talent show, sign up to sing one of your favorite worship songs.

Jesus' Family Tree
Matthew 1:1-17

"This is the genealogy of Jesus the Messiah the son of David, the son of Abraham." Matthew 1:1

I love family trees. I love being able to look back at my family's ancestors and see who I am related to. I find it fascinating to trace my family's heritage.

Because I love my own family tree, you know that I love to look at the family tree of Jesus. Matthew starts off his book by tracing back the family history of Jesus. Why do you think Matthew would do this? I think it was because he wanted us to see that Jesus could be traced back to King David and then also all the way back to Abraham. (You can find another family tree in Luke 3 that traces Jesus all the way back to Adam.)

Let's look at the names on the family tree of Jesus. There are some names that are hard to pronounce. Write down a few names that you think are hard to say: _____

_____

You may be tempted to skip over this part of Matthew, but take a few moments to search for some names you do recognize and write those names here: _____

_____

There are some important people in the lineage of Jesus. And maybe one or two that you are surprised to find there. An important thing to note here is that Jesus was known as the King of the Jews. The only way He could be known as a King on earth is if He was descended from a line of kings. And guess what? He was! Look at verse 6. Who is in His family tree that's listed as a king? You guessed it! It's King David. And because David was a king we know that those listed after him in this family tree were kings too. Jesus came from a long line of kings!

Maybe your family tree isn't like Jesus' and filled with some well-known people or royalty. But, your family tree is just as important. And why is it important? Because not only are you a child of your parents, but you are a child of God (1 John 3:1). You have a big family since you are a part of God's family. Remember how much God loves you and cares for you. And remember that He knows your name and knows everything about you because He loves you.

Follow Me

Ask your parents to help you write down your family tree. Thank God for your family members. Say a prayer for those who are still living.

Loving God, thank You for my family tree. I am so thankful to also be a part of Your family. Help me to always follow You and remember that You love me. In Jesus' name, Amen.

Breakfast Casserole

1 pkg. pork sausage
10 eggs, beaten
3 cups milk
2 tsp. dry mustard
1 tsp. salt

6 cups cubed bread
8 oz. shredded sharp cheese
½ tsp. black pepper
½ cup green onions, chopped

Preheat oven to 325°. In a large skillet, brown sausage over medium high heat. In a large bowl, combine eggs, milk, dry mustard, and salt. Spread half the bread evenly in a greased 9x13 pan. Sprinkle with half the pepper, half the cheese, half the sausage, and half the onions. Repeat the layers. Pour egg mixture over casserole. Bake uncovered for 1 hour. If casserole begins to brown too quickly, you may put aluminum foil on top and put back in oven.

Something To Chew On

. . . .

What would you serve Jesus for breakfast if He came over to your house today?

Joseph's Dream
Matthew 1:18-25

"When Joseph woke up, he did what the angel of the Lord had commanded him and took Mary home as his wife." Matthew 1:24

Ever had a dream where you woke up from your sleep and remembered every single detail about it?

God spoke to Joseph in a dream that we read about in Matthew 1. And I believe he woke up from that dream remembering every detail. Why? Because it was a dream in which God had spoken to him. You see, Joseph had just found out Mary was pregnant, but he knew it was not his child because they were not married yet. He was ready to let Mary go and not go through with marrying her.

But then God intervened.

An angel came to Joseph in a dream. The angel told him not to be afraid to take Mary as his wife. Joseph, I'm sure, was a little freaked out by all that was going on. He didn't want the attention for Mary, much less himself. I wonder if he thought about what others would say about him and Mary. What would they think about all this?

How many times have you been afraid to do something because you're afraid of what people will think about you if you do it?

Fear of what others think has stopped me from moving forward at times. I don't want to stand out in the crowd. I don't want others to talk about me or make fun of me or even question why I'm doing something. I just want to blend in.

I have had to face that fear head on in my life, too. God has shown me there is only one person I need to worry about pleasing and that is Him. Nobody else's opinion matters. Only His.

If you are facing a situation where you are afraid, especially of what others will think if you do it, I encourage you to let go. Remember that Jesus is with you. And ask God to help you be bold to do what He wants you to do, no matter what anyone else says.

Father, help me to let go of my fear of what others will think and walk boldly in my faith. Give me the same courage that You gave Joseph. In Jesus' name, Amen.

Follow Me

Stand out in the crowd today. Be bold and share the love of Jesus to others. This could be something like playing with someone on the playground that no one else likes to play with. Or perhaps you could stand out today at home by being kind to your brother or sister (maybe even offering to do one of their chores for them).

My Son, the Savior
Matthew 1:20-21

"She will give birth to a son, and you are to give him the name Jesus, because he will save his people from their sins." Matthew 1:21

I have two daughters. As their mom, I am super proud of them. I am proud of how well they do in school, how hard they work at playing soccer, how kind they are to their friends, and how they love Jesus and show His love to others. What can I say…I am a proud mom.

And I know that your parents are proud of you, too! I am sure you do and say many great things and make your parents so proud to call you their child. (Go right now and give your mom or dad a big hug and tell them thank you for being an awesome parent.)

I believe Joseph had to be a little proud when he found out that Jesus was going to be his son on this earth. Remember that Joseph was almost ready to leave Mary, but the angel came to visit him in a dream. The angel spoke to him the words we find in the verse above in Matthew 1:21: "She will give birth to a son, and you are to give him the name Jesus, because he will save his people from their sins."

Can you imagine what Joseph must have been thinking when he woke up from that dream? *My son, whom I am raising, is going to be the Son of God and He is going to save all people from their sins! How is this even possible? I don't know, but I sure am proud to be His earthly father! I get to be a father to the Savior of the world! How cool is that!*

Okay, so maybe he wasn't exactly thinking those thoughts, but I am sure behind the fear inside him was gratefulness that God chose him to raise His child on this earth. A child that was going to be a Savior for all people. A child that would be the King of Kings, the Lord of Lords. And what a proud parent Joseph would be.

Father God, thank You for my parents. Help me to always follow Your ways and listen to You. In Jesus' name, Amen.

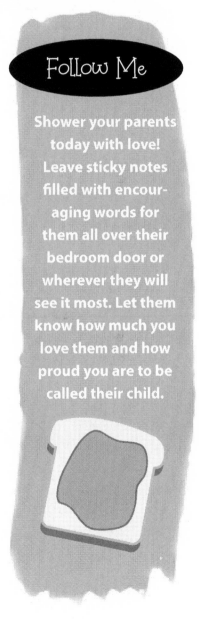

Follow Me

Shower your parents today with love! Leave sticky notes filled with encouraging words for them all over their bedroom door or wherever they will see it most. Let them know how much you love them and how proud you are to be called their child.

The Prophecy Fulfilled
Matthew 1:22-23

"All this took place to fulfill what the Lord had said through the prophet: 'The virgin will conceive and give birth to a son, and they will call him Immanuel' (which means 'God with us')." Matthew 1:22-23

Have you ever had to wait a long time for something to happen? Maybe you had to wait hours or days, or even months or years. But I don't believe that any of you have had to wait as long as the Israelites did for something to happen.

In Old Testament times the prophecy about Jesus Christ being born had been spoken by the prophet Isaiah. A prophecy is telling of something that will happen in the future. Did you know there were more than 700 years between the time Isaiah said this and the time that Jesus was actually born? That's a really long time!

Isaiah's prophecy is found in Isaiah 7:14: "Therefore the Lord himself will give you a sign: The virgin will conceive and give birth to a son, and will call him Immanuel."

Let's imagine for a second that we were one of the Israelites. We may have started out excited about this birth of a Savior, but as the years went by, we may have given up any hope of it ever happening. Why did God promise something if it was never going to happen?

But then it happened. Mary is filled with the Holy Spirit and she conceives and gives birth to a son. And His name is Immanuel, which means "God with us." (Remember how Jesus has many names that describe Him, and Immanuel is one of them).

God's promise is fulfilled! He wasn't joking with us. He didn't lie to us. He didn't go back on what He told us many, many years ago. He came through for us. He made good on His promise. He gave us a Savior. And His name is Jesus.

Father God, thank You for the promise of a Savior. Thank You for sending Your Son to this earth for us. Help us to continue to be faithful in our waiting. In Jesus' name, Amen.

Follow Me

Do you know what I find so helpful to do while I wait for something to happen? I pray about it. Think about what you are waiting for. Maybe that's for a grade on a test, for your sister or brother to forgive you, for your parents to give you what they promised, or maybe even for the arrival of your new brother or sister. No matter what you wait for, remember to pray and ask God to help you be patient while you wait.

Joseph Obeys

Matthew 1:24

"When Joseph woke up, he did what the angel of the
Lord had commanded him and took Mary home as his
wife." Matthew 1:24

There are so many people who tell you what to do, right? Let's think about who those people are. Your parents tell you what to do, and you are to listen and obey them as one of the Ten Commandments says. If you play a sport, then your coach tells you what to do, and you listen to them, especially if you want to get better in your sport. Maybe you have friends or siblings that like to tell you what to do…sometimes that can be good or bad. We also have to obey the law, as it's there to protect us and keep us safe. People tell us what to do because they are trying to teach us how to do something, or because they know what's best for us, or because it's the law and we must follow it.

But there's One whom we should listen to all the time…and that is God.

In this Scripture in Matthew, the Bible says that after Joseph woke from his sleep, "he did what the angel of the Lord had commanded him." (Matthew 1:24). I wonder what thoughts were going through Joseph's mind when he woke up. Did he question his dream? Did he wonder if God really had spoken to him?

I don't believe he had any doubts. I believe Joseph had a strong feeling he was to obey God after he woke up from his dream. I believe he knew for sure what he was to do. And he did it. Joseph took

Mary as his wife and he named him Jesus. Joseph obeyed what the Lord asked of him.

Have you recently had that strong feeling God has asked you to do something? Have you listened, or have you been hesitant? Whether it's a big thing or a small thing, I encourage you to take that step forward. Trust God and remember that all we need to do is obey Him.

Dear Lord, help me to obey You in all I do, whether big or small. Remind me that You know what's best for me and help me to fully trust in You. In Jesus' name, Amen.

Follow Me

God says in the Ten Commandments, "Honor your father and your mother." (Exodus 20:12). Today, make it your mission to obey all your parents ask you to do. And do it without complaining. You will definitely see a big smile on your parents' faces when you do what they ask.

No Room

Luke 2:6-7

"While they were there, the time came for the baby to be born, and she gave birth to her firstborn, a son. She wrapped him in cloths and placed him in a manger, because there was no guest room available for them." Luke 2:6-7

What would your parents do if they were planning a vacation? They would probably search the internet or make phone calls and research where you'd be going. Probably one of the first things they would do is reserve a place to stay at a hotel or a condo. You must have a place to sleep wherever you are going. I couldn't imagine traveling to a city and not know where I would be staying. But that's exactly what Mary and Joseph did when they went to Bethlehem.

Back in the days of the birth of Jesus, there were no phones. There was no internet. There was no website to use to get the best deal on a place to stay in Bethlehem. There was no way to call ahead and book a room to stay for a night.

More than likely, though, the inn in this story was not anything like a hotel. It was actually a house. When people travelled, they stayed in the homes of relatives. One of Joseph's ancestors was King David and he was from Bethlehem. So we can safely assume there were plenty of relatives they could have stayed with. But maybe their journey took way longer than expected, as one would think it would when travelling with a nine-month pregnant woman. So when they got to Bethlehem, the family members they could have stayed with already had people staying with them. Their homes were full and there was no guest room available for them.

But there was one home, one person, who gave them a place to stay. It wasn't likely that it was a stable as we think about today. Many people had caves behind their homes where animals stayed. That is where Mary and Joseph stayed for the night and where she delivered the Savior of the world.

The world had no room for Jesus that night. What about you? Do you leave room for Jesus in your life? Or is your day so crammed with activities, school, and fun that there is not a single space of time dedicated to Jesus? I am guilty of this for sure. Time gets away from me and I have forgotten to leave room for Jesus. Let's promise each other that we will carve out time in our day to spend with Him. Let's leave a lot of room for Jesus every day.

Jesus, forgive me when I don't spend time with You daily. Help me to always make room for You each day. Amen.

Follow Me

Clean out your room today. Get rid of all the toys you don't play with or clothes you don't wear anymore. Donate them to someone in need or give to a thrift store.

12

The Birth of Jesus
Luke 2:1-7

"And she gave birth to her firstborn, a son. She wrapped him in cloths and laid him in a manger, because there was no guest room available for them." Luke 2:7

Where do mothers go when it's time for a baby to be born?

If you said a hospital, you would be correct. Hospitals have all the things you need for a safe delivery of a baby: doctors, nurses, medicine, beds, blankets, pillows, heating and air, and even a television! However, back in the day when it was time for Jesus to be born, Mary and Joseph didn't make it to a hospital. There wasn't even such a thing as a hospital back then. So where did Mary go when it was time to deliver baby Jesus?

Remember they had finally found a place to stay. It wasn't exactly a nice place, either. There were animals all around and it had lots of hay. I am sure the smell of the cave was overwhelming at times. No comfy bed for Mary to lay her head. No fluffy blankets or pillows. No heat or air. And definitely not a television. There wasn't even a real bed to put baby Jesus in! Not exactly a place where you would think God's Son would be born, right?

But it was the perfect place. The most humble place. A place where the Savior of the world, the Prince of Peace, the Lord of Lords, the Messiah, the Christ, came to be with us on this earth. Jesus didn't need anything fancy. He didn't need a big bed. He didn't even need a real room. He entered the world in the way God wanted Him to… in a peaceful, humble way.

I couldn't think of a better place for Jesus to be born.

Prince of Peace, remind me of the humble way You entered the world so I can always put others needs before mine. In Jesus' name, Amen.

Follow Me

Do you know someone that just had a baby? Make them a congratulations card and send to them. Maybe even include in there a special note just for the baby…something he or she could read when they get older.

Bagel Dip

8 oz. cream cheese
½ cup mayo
1 cup grated Swiss cheese

2 Tbsp. chopped green onions
8 slices bacon, cooked and crumbled
½ cup Ritz crackers, crushed

Set out cream cheese to soften. In a medium bowl, stir together mayo, Swiss cheese, and green onions. Add in the cream cheese and the cooked and crumbled bacon. Stir until well blended. Put mixture into a baking dish. Sprinkle crackers on top. Bake at 350° for 20 minutes. Serve with any type of bagel.

Something To Chew On

. . . .

**What is one question you have always
wanted to ask Jesus?**

The Shepherds and Angels
Luke 2:8–20

"Glory to God in the highest heaven, and on earth peace to those on whom his favor rests." Luke 2:14

"Isn't there anyone who can tell me what Christmas is all about?"

That's the question Charlie Brown asks in the movie *A Charlie Brown Christmas.* He wanted to know what the true meaning of Christmas was. That's when his friend, Linus, steps up to the plate. Linus takes center stage and delivers the message found in our Scripture reading today.

Christmas is not about Santa Claus, lights, Christmas trees, presents, caroling, or feasts. Our world has added all these things into the holiday. And even though these are wonderful and fun ways to celebrate, these are not what the true meaning of Christmas is all about.

Christmas is about celebrating the birth of our Savior, Jesus Christ. An angel kicked off the night of celebration by visiting the shepherds in the field who were watching over their sheep. I can only imagine the fear that came over them as this heavenly being shone over them with the greatest light they had ever seen. The angel delivered good news of great joy and told the shepherds exactly how they would find this baby boy who is the Messiah. Then out of nowhere came this…

"Suddenly a great company of the heavenly host appeared with the angel, praising God and saying, 'Glory to God in the highest heaven, and on earth peace to those on whom his favor rests.'" (Luke 2:13-14)

One angel was quite a shock, but then to have a multitude of angels must have been overwhelming. And they were singing with the most beautiful voices one had ever heard. This wasn't just any song, but it was a song of praise. They were praising God and giving glory to Him. The angels were celebrating and praising the birth of our Savior. Glory to God!

Holy God, forgive me when I get so caught up in the hustle and bustle of Christmas that I forget the true meaning of this holiday. Help me to remember Jesus at all times. Amen.

Follow Me

Watch *A Charlie Brown Christmas*. Memorize Linus' part when he gets on stage and tells everyone what the true meaning of Christmas is all about (Luke 2:8-14). Share that message with a friend today.

Hurry Up, Don't Delay
Luke 2:15-18

"Let's go to Bethlehem and see this thing that has happened, which the Lord has told us about." Luke 2:15b

I am not a slow person. I like to do everything fast: talk fast, eat fast, walk fast. I am not a person to procrastinate because I like to get things done…fast. If there is a project to do, then I am on it. I don't wait around. I am not one to sit still, but am always moving and going and doing something. If I sit still too long, then you know what I do? I fall asleep! My brain and body are wired to be on the move.

The night Jesus was born there was a group of people who also moved fast and didn't want to wait around. Those people were the shepherds. The angel had just delivered the good news of the birth of Jesus, who is the Messiah. Despite their shock, they moved quickly. I love that the shepherds didn't waste time. They had just been given word from the angel of the arrival of the Messiah. They couldn't keep still and wait till morning. They had to get there fast and see the baby born to save everyone.

After they saw Jesus, they left and went to tell everyone they could find. They could not keep the birth of Jesus a secret. This was not something to be kept to themselves. It was a message everyone needed to hear. The angel had said this news was for all people. God chose them to be the messengers and spread the word about the birth of this baby boy, our Savior.

I encourage each of you to be like the shepherds. Go now and tell someone about Jesus. That not only includes your family and friends, but even people you don't know. Sometimes you don't have to say words, your actions will show Jesus, too.

Hurry up! Don't delay! Go tell someone about Jesus today!

Glorious Father, help me not to keep Your message of Jesus to myself. Use me to be Your messenger and let others know the amazing things You have done for me. In Jesus' name, Amen.

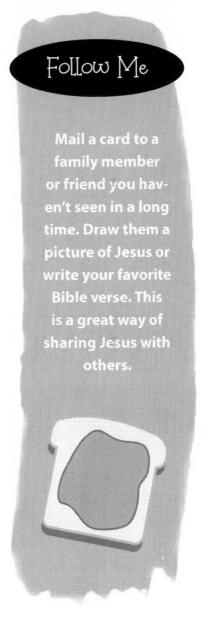

Follow Me

Mail a card to a family member or friend you haven't seen in a long time. Draw them a picture of Jesus or write your favorite Bible verse. This is a great way of sharing Jesus with others.

Simeon's Bucket List

Luke 2:25-35

"It had been revealed to him by the Holy Spirit that he would not die before he had seen the Lord's Messiah."
Luke 2:26

Bucket lists are fun to make. I have seen kids and adults write down a list of things they want to do one day. Some of the items on a list could be places they want to go, visiting every state in the United States, learning how to do something new like play the guitar, doing something adventurous like skydiving or bungee jumping, or maybe even something as simple as giving encouragement to someone each day.

The idea to make a bucket list is something pretty new, so it definitely was not "a thing" back in the day when Jesus was born. But I would venture to say that if there was, then a man named Simeon would have put on his bucket list, "See the Messiah."

Simeon is a man only mentioned once in the Bible. The Bible says Simeon was "righteous and devout." (Luke 2:25). That means he was a man who loved God and was devoted to serving Him. The Holy Spirit had laid it on his heart that he wouldn't die until he had seen Jesus, the Messiah.

One day he felt a prompting to go to the temple. It was the Holy Spirit that gave him that prompting. I have a feeling he wasn't sure why he was supposed to go to the temple that day. He didn't know what would happen. But when Mary and Joseph brought Jesus into the temple, then Simeon had to be bursting with joy. He took one look and knew this baby was the Messiah, the One sent from God to save us.

Simeon was so overwhelmed with excitement that he took Jesus into his arms and began praising God. I like to picture Simeon holding Jesus high up, dancing around the temple, maybe even rocking Him back and forth. God had promised Simeon that he would see the Messiah and God kept His promise. Here he was holding the Messiah in his arms and praising the Lord. I even like to imagine that Simeon probably shed some tears too. He was so overjoyed, and he couldn't help but let happy tears roll down his face.

God is the One who always keeps His promises. You can read throughout the whole Bible about times when God has never failed and has always made good on the promises He makes with His people. The best promise was the promise of a Savior. He delivered that promise in the birth of Jesus Christ. And Simeon was blessed to have gotten to see Him and hold Him. Praise be to God.

Everlasting Lord, thank You for the promise of sending us Jesus. Help me to remember to always follow You and never doubt Your love for me. In Jesus' name, Amen.

Follow Me

Make a "Faith Bucket List." Write down things you want to do that have to do with Jesus and your faith. Some things might be: reading a chapter of the Bible each day, going to church every Sunday, singing in the choir, praying for other people or going on a mission trip.

The Wise Men
Matthew 2:1-12

"On coming to the house, they saw the child with his mother Mary, and they bowed down and worshiped him. Then they opened their treasures and presented him with gifts of gold, frankincense, and myrrh." Matthew 2:11

When a mother-to-be is expecting the arrival of a new baby, one of the things she does is create a baby registry at a store (like Target or Walmart). She picks out things she would like for her new baby. Some things she might register for are clothes, toys, stroller, car seat, crib, baby bathtub, bibs, bottles, pacifiers, blankets, and lots of other fun things. She does this because friends will give a baby shower for her and the guests invited to the shower can go to the store, pull up her baby registry, and purchase items that she wants for her new baby. It's a great way to help new parents prepare for the arrival of their child.

We know there was no such thing as a baby registry when Jesus was born. But, even if Mary did have a baby registry, I am pretty sure she would have never registered for gold, frankincense, or myrrh. What would you do with those gifts for a baby? Those three items are the gifts that the wise men (also called Magi) brought to baby Jesus when they found Him. They had heard that a king had been born and they were on a mission to find Him so they could deliver gifts and worship Him.

In order to find Him, they followed the bright, shining star in the sky that landed on a house in Bethlehem. When they arrived they were so excited because they had finally found the King of the Jews.

They immediately bowed down and worshiped Him and presented Him with the finest gifts they could bring: gold, frankincense, and myrrh. These were gifts they felt were fit for a king.

Did you know Jesus was actually God's gift to us? God sent us the best gift we could ever get. Because of Jesus, we can live forever with Him in heaven if we believe in Him. When the wise men came to give gifts to Jesus, I'm not sure if they understood that Jesus was actually a gift for all of us from God. But we know today that He is the greatest gift ever!

God of All, thank You for sending Jesus. Help me to remember that He is a gift from You and to always trust in Him. Amen.

Follow Me

On a piece of paper, write down three gifts you can give to Jesus today. Some of those gifts might be your heart, love for other people, showing kindness, or helping those in need. Then take that piece of paper and wrap it in a box. Put it in your room to remind yourself of the gifts you have given to Jesus.

Jesus as a Child
Luke 2:41-52

*"After three days they found him in the temple courts,
sitting among the teachers, listening to them and asking
them questions." Luke 2:46*

Have you ever gotten lost from your parents? It can be a scary moment for sure.

I remember a time when I was young that I got mad at my mom when we were shopping at a mall. I decided to go away from her and pout about it. When I finished pouting, I turned around and could not find her. I can remember the panic I felt when I didn't know where she was. This nice woman saw me crying and she helped me find my mom. She was in the store right near where I had been standing. I was so grateful to be reunited with my mom that day!

There was a time as a child that Jesus got separated from His parents. Do you think He cried or was upset? His reaction was actually the opposite of mine. He wasn't worried at all. It was His parents (Mary and Joseph) who were extremely upset. It took them three days to find Him!

And do you know where they found Jesus? In the temple listening to the teachers and asking them questions. His parents were so worried about Him because they could not find Him, but when they found Jesus, He acted surprised they were worried about Him. Didn't they know He would be in His Father's house?

After Mary and Joseph found Jesus, it says He went back with them to Nazareth (where they lived) and He was obedient to them. He listened to them and honored His mother and father. And you know what it says after that? It says: "And Jesus grew in wisdom and stature, and in favor with God and man." (Luke 2:52). As Jesus got older, He became wiser and found favor with God.

My prayer for you is that you will be obedient to your parents. Listen to what they say. Do as they ask you to do. They love you and want the best for you. And when you do, I believe you will grow in wisdom, just as Jesus did.

Father God, help me to listen to my parents even when I don't want to. Forgive me for the times I am disobedient to them and disobedient to You. Help me to grow wise, just as Jesus did. Amen.

Follow Me

Practice your listening skills today. Pay more attention to what your parents say and do. Pay attention to what your friends are telling you. Be a good listener today.

Be a Witness

John 1:6–8

"He came as a witness to testify concerning that light, so that through him all might believe." John 1:7

When I was a kid, my parents gave me chores to do: unload the dishwasher, set the table, take out the trash, and mow the lawn. I can remember my mother having to remind me to do these things too. I didn't always remember to do these things when it was time… probably because I truly did not enjoy doing these things so I would just "happen" to forget to do them. But don't worry…my mother never let me forget!

Maybe you have chores too. Things around the house that your parents make you do. If you are like me then you may have several chores to do. And they aren't always fun, are they?

There was a man named John the Baptist who was given a job by God. He didn't have multiple jobs to do (like you and I are given by our parents). John had only one job. And do you know what that job was? Let's go read John 1:7 to find out (see verse above).

This verse says that John came as a witness to testify to who Jesus was. His job was to make the name of Jesus known to everyone. Other verses in the Bible say that he came to "prepare the way of the Lord." He was letting everyone know the Messiah (Jesus) was coming. You see…the Jews had been waiting a very long time for the Messiah. It had been 700 years since God had spoken through Isaiah and promised He would send Jesus to the earth. Some people may have even given up hope that God would keep His promise.

But God did keep His promise, because Jesus was born on the earth. And God gave John the Baptist the job of letting everyone know Jesus was coming. His ministry on earth would be starting soon so get ready! Aren't you glad that John the Baptist listened to God and did the one job God asked him to do?

Everlasting God, thank You for sending John the Baptist to prepare the way of the Lord. Help me to be like him and be a witness to other people and let others know about You. In Jesus' name, Amen.

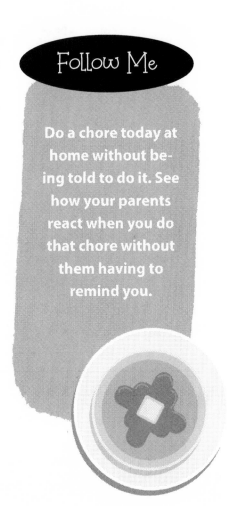

Follow Me

Do a chore today at home without being told to do it. See how your parents react when you do that chore without them having to remind you.

Monkey Bread

2 cans refrigerated biscuits   1 ½ cup sugar
2 tsp. cinnamon   1 stick butter

Cut biscuits in fourths. In a mixing bowl add together biscuits, ½ cup sugar and 1 tsp. cinnamon. Shake together, making sure biscuits are coated well.

Grease a Bundt cake pan with butter or spray. Add coated biscuits to pan.

Melt butter. Mix with 1 cup sugar and 1 tsp. cinnamon. Pour over the biscuits in the Bundt cake pan.

Bake at 350° for 35 minutes. Cool for a few minutes then turn monkey bread out of pan and serve warm.

Something To Chew On

· · · · · · · · · · · · · · · · · ·

**What ways has God has blessed your life
with laughter this week?**

The Baptism of Jesus
Matthew 3:13-17

*"And a voice from heaven said, 'This is my Son, whom I
love; with him I am well pleased.'" Matthew 3:17*

Doesn't it feel good to have your parents tell you they are pleased with you or they are proud of you? I think it's safe to say that you probably do love when they say that. We all like to have the approval of our parents. And we all like for our parents to be pleased with everything we do.

We read about this same type of thing in the third chapter of Matthew when Jesus was grown and it was time for Him to start His ministry. Remember that John the Baptist was preparing the way for Jesus to begin His ministry and letting everyone know He was coming. Before Jesus began His ministry, He wanted to be baptized by John the Baptist. He found John at the Jordan River and asked him to baptize Him. Of course, John didn't feel worthy enough to baptize Jesus. In fact, he asked Jesus to baptize him! But Jesus told John that he needed to baptize Him.

As soon as Jesus came up out of the water, we read, "At that moment heaven was opened, and he saw the Spirit of God descending like a dove and alighting on him." (Matthew 3:16).

Then it happened. God's voice came from heaven and spoke these words for everyone there to hear, "This is my Son, whom I love; with him I am well pleased." (Matthew 3:17).

I like to imagine that when Jesus heard these words spoken to Him by God that a big smile came across His face. His Heavenly

Father just said that He was pleased with Him. I believe that He felt the love of His Father that day and that made Him smile. I know I would be smiling big, too, if I was Him.

Remember that even if your earthly parents don't tell you they are pleased with you, know that your Heavenly Father is. God loves you unconditionally, which means that no matter what you do, He will always love you. Sometimes it helps to say Scripture out loud to really make it sink in so say this verse but insert your name.

This is my (son/daughter), (your name), whom I love; with (him/her) I am well pleased.

I hope that by speaking that verse out loud, you know that you are loved by God and He is pleased with you!

Father God, thank You for my parents. Help me to remember that no matter what I say or do, You love me and are pleased with me. I love You, God. Amen.

Follow Me

What could you do that would make your parents happy? Perhaps you could clean your room, share your toys with your sibling, be kind to that same sibling, or even just be polite and show good manners. Whatever you believe would please them today...do it.

Into the Wilderness

Matthew 4:1–11

"Then Jesus was led by the Spirit into the wilderness to be tempted by the devil." Matthew 4:1

What are some things that you are tempted by? Maybe you're tempted to eat a 5-pound bag of candy all at one time. Maybe you didn't study for a test and you're tempted to look at your friend's paper for the answers so you can make a good grade. Maybe you're tempted to hit your brother or sister because they were being mean to you. Maybe you're tempted not to do what your parents asked you to do because you're busy playing video games. We are tempted to do so many things. But how many times do you actually do the things you're tempted to do?

Remember from our last devotion that Jesus was baptized by John the Baptist. Right after this, He goes into the wilderness where He fasts for forty days and forty nights. This type of fasting Jesus did meant that He did not eat any food. Instead, He spent His time focused on God and He prayed. After the fasting is over, Satan comes and tempts Him. Basically, Satan is tempting Jesus to turn away from God and instead follow him.

Do you know how Jesus fought this temptation and instead kept His focus on God?

Every time Satan tempted Him to do something, He fought back using God's Word. After Satan tempts Him, Jesus says, "It is written." That means that what He's about to say is written in the Bible. Jesus fought off temptation with Scripture. And guess what? Satan left

Him alone and went away from Him because Satan didn't win. (Can I get a loud scream and lots of cheering?)

When you are tempted to do something you know you shouldn't do, remember you can fight off that temptation by using God's Word, just like Jesus did. That's why it's so important to read the Bible so you can know what God says and what God wants you to do. Here's an example:

Tempted to say a mean word to someone you don't like? Remember Ephesians 4:32:

"Be kind and compassionate to one another, forgiving each other, just as in Christ God forgave you."

Tempted to turn your back on a friend because they were mean to you? Remember John 13:34:

"Love one another. As I have loved you, so you must love one another."

Remember to read your Bible so you can know what God says and fight off temptations!

Lord of All, help me to do as You want me to do. Help me to read Your Word daily so I can draw closer to You. Thank You for giving me the Bible so I can know more about You. Amen.

Follow Me

Today when you are tempted to do things or say things you know you shouldn't, do what is right. Turn the temptation to do something bad into doing something good.

Come, Follow Me

Mark 1:16–20

*"'Come, follow me,' Jesus said, 'and I will send you out to
fish for people.'" Mark 1:17*

Fish for *people*? What is Jesus talking about?

This verse in the book of Mark might have you wondering why
Jesus would tell the men He is calling to be His disciples to fish for
people. You don't fish for people; you fish for fish! Right?

I believe here that Jesus is talking the language of these fishermen. The one thing they knew how to do well was fish. They knew
exactly what it took to catch a fish. Back in their times, they didn't
have fishing poles. They used nets mostly. Maybe even spears or
hooks, too. Being a fisherman is also a difficult job. It's not always
easy to catch fish.

Jesus knew these men had what it took to be part of His mission in catching people for God. When Jesus said they would fish
for people, He meant they would be going out and telling people
about Him, about how He came to save them from their sins, about
how much He loves them, and getting them to follow after God.

Just like it was difficult being a fisherman, it would also be difficult to fish for people. Jesus would be teaching them and showing
them what it meant to live for God. He would be living His life in a
way that would be an example for not only His disciples, but for all
people.

Jesus called not only the disciples to follow Him, but He also calls
you and me. It doesn't matter how old you are, Jesus can use you

to help Him fish for people. You can share His love with others at school, at home, or even at Walmart!

Don't think that because you are a young child that you can't fish for people. He calls you, my dear child, to tell others about Him.

Will you come and follow Jesus with me?

Dear God, thank You for calling me to follow You. Help me to be an example to others of what it means to follow You. Show me the people that need to hear about Your love. Amen.

Follow Me

Leave a reminder about Jesus in your mailbox for your postal worker. Write out your favorite Bible verse on a sticky note and put that you are praying for them. Then place it inside your mailbox and put the flag up.

Water into Wine

John 2:1-12

"What Jesus did here in Cana of Galilee was the first of the signs through which he revealed his glory; and his disciples believed in him." John 2:11

Have you ever been to a wedding where they ran out of food or drinks? I can only imagine how embarrassing this would be to the bride and groom if it happened at their wedding!

This very thing happened to a wedding Jesus was attending with His disciples and His mother. They ran out of wine. Mary, Jesus' mother, asked Jesus to help because she believed He could. She believed in His power. She knew He could do something no one else could.

Jesus performed His first miracle that day. He had some servants fill up six stone jars with water. Each of those jars could hold up to 20-30 gallons of water (that's a lot of water!). The servants did as He said. But when they poured the drinks for the guests, it wasn't water anymore. It was wine!

Did you know that no one really knew this happened except a small group of people? It wasn't a miracle where thousands of people believed in Jesus because they saw Him do this amazing thing. Jesus' first miracle was really meant for only a small group of people to see. And this miracle revealed who He was to His closest of followers -- His disciples.

What Jesus did was amazing and miraculous. But it wasn't time for everyone to know exactly who He was. He performed a miracle but didn't make a big scene. He didn't shout out to everyone that He had just saved the bride and groom from complete embarrassment because they had run out of wine. The miracle He performed was actually pretty amazing, but it was done in a quiet way because He wasn't ready to reveal who He was just yet.

Jesus calls each of us to help one another. This could be in small or big ways. But one thing we need to remember is that when we do something for someone else, we don't need to make a big deal about it. We don't need to wait around to make sure someone notices what we did. We don't help others so we can be praised. We help others so that God can be praised. Today, do something to help another person. And if someone thanks you or praises you for it, say "Thanks be to God!"

Dear God, thank You for the miracles that Jesus did on this earth. Help me to show Your love to others and to always give You the praise for all things. I love You, Lord. Amen.

Follow Me

Make a lemonade stand in your neighborhood. But don't charge for the lemonade...give it away for free. Be a blessing to your neighbors today by giving them something to drink.

Born Again

John 3:1–21

"For God so loved the world that he gave his one and only Son, that whoever believes in him shall not perish but have eternal life." John 3:16

In John chapter 3, we find Jesus talking with a Pharisee (a religious leader) named Nicodemus. Nicodemus had some questions he wanted to ask Jesus, but he couldn't do that during the day because he was afraid of his fellow Pharisees. They might punish him if they saw him talking to Jesus. So Nicodemus came at night and told Jesus that he knew that He was from God.

Then Jesus said to Nicodemus, "Very truly I tell you, no one can see the kingdom of God unless they are born again." (John 3:3). This confused Nicodemus. He couldn't understand how someone could be born a second time.

Jesus goes on to explain that He didn't mean a person could physically be born a second time. He was talking about being born again in the spirit. And being born in the spirit means doing exactly what John 3:16 says. When we believe that Jesus is God's Son, that He came to this earth to die for our sins, and that He forgives us of all the bad things we have done, then we will receive eternal life. And eternal life means that when we die, we will go to heaven and live forever with God.

The decision to accept Jesus and follow Him is the most important decision you will ever make. It affects your life after you leave this earth. I pray each of you will make that decision to accept Jesus as your Savior. I want to see each of you in heaven one day. I want to spend eternal life with all of you. And God wants to spend forever with you and all of His children.

That's why it's so important to tell others of Jesus and His love for them. We want everyone on this earth to know how awesome God is and how amazing it is that Jesus came to save us so we could live forever with Him. Go out today and tell someone else about Jesus!

Father God, I am so grateful that Jesus came to die for all of us so that we could live forever with You. Help me to share that same love with someone else today. In Jesus' name, Amen.

Follow Me

Memorize John 3:16. This verse will be one you can share with others who don't know Jesus. Need help memorizing it? Check out a YouTube video by Jump-Start3 on John 3:16.

The Woman at the Well

John 4:1-26

"Jesus answered, 'Everyone who drinks this water will be thirsty again, but whoever drinks the water I give them will never thirst. Indeed, the water I give them will become in them a spring of water welling up to eternal life.'"
John 4:13-14

Has anyone ever offered you a cup of living water? Probably not. What do you think your reaction would be if someone did? You might ask them to repeat what they said because you would want to make sure you heard them right. Perhaps you'd let a "say what?" spill out of your mouth. Or maybe you would politely ask them what living water is because you have no idea what they are talking about.

Jesus came to a town in Samaria and sat by a well. It was around noon and a woman came to the well to draw water from it. He asked her for a drink because He was thirsty. Her response was one of surprise, for a couple of reasons. First, she was a woman and men did not speak to women in public unless it was their wife. Second, Jesus was a Jew and she was a Samaritan. Jews and Samaritans did not get along. They did not like each other one bit. So why in the world was this man talking to her? She couldn't believe it.

Then Jesus offers something to her that no one else has ever offered her before…living water. Her reaction might not have been the same as yours. She did ask Him several questions, though. However, one of them was not "what is living water?".

What exactly, then, is living water? Jesus is not talking literally about water that is alive and can breathe. Living water stands for Jesus and His gift of eternal life. Jesus is the living water and when we accept Him as our Savior, we are given the gift of eternal life. He gave this gift of living water to everyone. Even though Jews and Samaritans didn't get along, it didn't stop Jesus from sharing it with them. He wants everyone in the world to come to believe in Him.

And you know what? The Samaritan woman at the well that day with Jesus accepted this living water and His gift of eternal life. Isn't that amazing?!!

Living Water, thank You for the gift You have given to me. Help me to share this living water with everyone I meet so they can come to know You as I know You. In Jesus' name, Amen.

Follow Me

If your town hosts a road race or a festival, give bottles of water to those who attend. Share the love of Jesus and let them know Jesus loves them.

Sausage Balls

1 ½ cups Bisquick
1-pound mild sausage
1 stick sharp cheddar cheese, grated

Mix all 3 ingredients in a bowl using your hands. You can add more Bisquick if you like your sausage balls to have more breading. Make sure it's mixed together well. Roll the mixture into small balls. Place on a cookie sheet and bake at 375° for 10-12 minutes.

Something To Chew On

· · · · · · · · · · · · · · · ·

What is your favorite book of the
Bible and why?

The First Evangelist

John 4:27-42

"Many of the Samaritans from that town believed in him because of the woman's testimony." John 4:39

How cool would it be if a person came to believe in Jesus because of what you told them about Him? Maybe you tell them about a way He has helped you in your life, or even tell them a story about Jesus that's in the Bible. No matter what you tell them, if they came to believe in Jesus because of what you said, I believe you would feel so happy—overflowing with joy because of the way God led you to share His love with that person.

Well, that's exactly what happened in the story we read about yesterday of the woman at the well. She got so excited about all the things Jesus told her about herself (see verses 15-19) that she just had to tell someone else.

So she ran back to her town to share about Jesus. She was even so excited that she left her water jar behind – the one thing she came to the well to get. She then proceeded to tell everyone everything Jesus said to her. And because of what she said, they, too, believed in Jesus. They didn't have to see Jesus and hear Him for themselves, but they believed because of her testimony. That's pretty cool!

She's the first evangelist (a person who shares testimonies and stories about Jesus). Not even the disciples had told people yet about Jesus. They had just been following Jesus, learning from Him and listening to Him teach others. So the woman at the well was the very first person to share about Jesus with other people.

The Samaritans wanted to meet Jesus, too, so she took them back to the well and He taught them some more. And it says that even more people came to believe in Him. See how effective one person can be? All it takes is you sharing your faith in Jesus and that starts a ripple effect. And it keeps going and going and going.

Don't keep your faith in Jesus to yourself. Share it and watch others come to know Jesus, too.

Father God, thank You for giving Your life for me. Give me the courage to share with others about Your love. In Jesus' name, Amen.

Follow Me

Sometimes it helps to write down what you would say to someone about Jesus before you tell them. So grab a sheet of paper and write down what Jesus means to you. Tell about how He loves you and what He's done to help you through your life.

Jesus Heals the Sick
Matthew 4:23-25

"Jesus went throughout Galilee, teaching in their synagogues, proclaiming the good news of the kingdom, and healing every disease and sickness among the people."
Matthew 4:23

It's no fun being sick, is it? I don't like going to the doctor, but sometimes you must go if you want to get better. A doctor figures out what your illness is and treats you with medicine to get you feeling like yourself quickly.

Back in the time when Jesus was on the earth, there were doctors, but they did not have such a great understanding of the human body and all the illnesses like we do today. Their ability to treat an illness was probably more difficult than it is for a doctor today. Medicine has come a long way since Bible times.

So you can imagine that when word spread that Jesus could heal people instantly, crowds of people sought Him out so they could be made well. Matthew 4:24 says, "News about him spread all over Syria, and people brought to him all who were ill with various diseases, those suffering severe pain, the demon-possessed, those having seizures, and the paralyzed; and he healed them."

Anyone with any kind of illness flocked to Him so they could be healed. And we aren't talking just a few people, but large crowds of people. That's a lot of people! And they didn't make an appointment to be healed like we have to today in order to see a doctor. They just came to Jesus and He healed them.

Jesus was compassionate. When He saw the crowds of people coming from all over to be healed, He couldn't turn any of them away. He healed all of them because He had compassion for them. And He has compassion for you, too. He doesn't like to see us not feeling well. Even though we can't see Jesus today, He still heals us. Sometimes it's instantaneous, but other times it takes time.

Jesus uses doctors and nurses to heal us today, as well as medicines, too. Jesus is our Great Physician and He is still healing people today. I am so thankful for His care for us.

Great Physician, thank You for healing me when I am sick. Thank You for the doctors and nurses You provide to bring healing to me. Help me to feel You near me when I don't feel well. In Jesus' name, Amen.

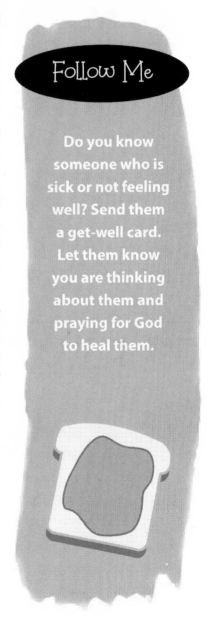

Follow Me

Do you know someone who is sick or not feeling well? Send them a get-well card. Let them know you are thinking about them and praying for God to heal them.

27

Jesus Prays Alone
Mark 1:25-29

"Very early in the morning, while it was still dark, Jesus got up, left the house and went off to a solitary place, where he prayed." Mark 1:35

Can you picture this scene in your mind? It's early morning. Too early for anyone to be doing anything. But Jesus is awake. He's up and already out the door. Maybe He's hungry and wanting to find some food. Maybe He couldn't sleep and just needed to take a walk. Maybe He just didn't want to be in that house.

Actually, none of these things are the reason Jesus left the house where He was staying early that morning. He left because He wanted to pray to God. He needed to find a place where He could be alone so He could talk to God. He just wanted to pray.

I believe each of us can learn something here from Jesus. There are times when we need to spend time alone with God. It just needs to be Him and us. And that means having to turn off all those things that distract us: video games, television, cell phones, tablets. These things keep us busy and take our focus off God.

You need to find a place in your house (or maybe somewhere outside in your yard) where you can be alone with God. Just the two of you. Nothing to distract you. And then just talk. Tell God what is on your heart. Share with Him the good things and bad things. He wants you to talk with Him. And remember that when you do talk to Him, He hears you. God is always listening.

Dear God, thank You for the example Jesus provides for me. Help me to spend time alone with You daily. Thank You for always listening to me and hearing my prayers. In Jesus' name, Amen.

Follow Me

Starting your day off with Jesus is a great way to help you get through the day. If you're not a morning person, make it a point to set your alarm for enough time so you can spend time with Jesus before you must get ready for school. Try waking up early for one week and see how you do. It may seem early to you, but I promise the more you do it, the easier it will be to get up.

28

Because You Say So

Luke 5:1-11

"Simon answered, 'Master, we've worked hard all night and haven't caught anything. But because you say so, I will let down the nets.'" Luke 5:5

What happens if you try to do something one way and it doesn't work? You might try again, but after a couple of times, you see that it's not going to work, and you give up. What's the point in doing it that way if it's not going to work, right?

In Luke 5, we get a little more detail about the day that Jesus called His disciples to follow Him and fish for people. Simon Peter, Andrew, James, and John are on the shore of the Sea of Galilee cleaning their nets. Jesus climbs aboard and asks Peter to go out a little way so He can teach the people. After He's done, He asks Peter to throw his net over the side of the boat to catch some fish.

But you see, Peter and his friends had been working hard all day and night and hadn't caught anything. Why would they throw their net over the boat again when they had just spent the whole day doing that and got nothing?

Peter surprises us though and agrees to do what Jesus asked him to do. He utters four words that tell us he's actually going to listen to what Jesus told him to do…"because you say so." (Luke 5:5b).

Why do you think Peter did it? I think it's because he had been listening to Jesus teach and knew He was wise. He had heard and seen that Jesus could do some amazing things, so why not give it one more try (although in the back of his mind he may have been thinking it was a dumb idea).

And guess what happened? Peter caught so many fish that the net started to break! How could that be possible? He had worked hard all day and not caught anything but now when Jesus tells him to do it, he catches more than his net can handle. It was crazy!

Here's what I want you to take away from this story… Jesus is going to call you to do great things for Him. Sometimes those things might sound bizarre. Or they might even be something you tried to do or say before and it didn't work out. But when you feel Jesus telling you to do something…do it. Why should you do it? Because He says so.

God of All Things, thank You for calling me. Help me to listen to You. Help me not to question what You ask me to do, but to just do it. Thank You for loving me. In Jesus' name, Amen.

Follow Me

Take some paper and a marker and trace your feet. On each foot, write down things you feel Jesus calls you to do. Those could be things like be kind, listen better, read my Bible, pray more, or make people smile. Hang these on your wall in your bedroom leading the feet up to a sign that says: "Because You Say So: Luke 5:5." That will be a visual reminder for you to remember to follow Jesus and do what He's called you to do.

The Beatitudes

Matthew 5:1-12

"Now when Jesus saw the crowds, he went up on a mountainside and sat down. His disciples came to him, and he began to teach them." Matthew 5:1-2

In one of our previous devotions, large crowds of people were flocking to Jesus so they could be healed of their diseases. Jesus saw a great opportunity here to teach these people. When large amounts of people are following you, wouldn't you want to use the time they are with you to let others know about God?

Jesus recognized this as a time to begin a great teaching. He wanted so many people to come to know God and to follow Him. So He went up on a mountain and began teaching what we have come to know as the Sermon on the Mount. He's basically teaching them about how to live a godly life.

The first part of this sermon is something that we call "The Beatitudes." Beatitudes are "special sayings of Jesus. They explain how to be blessed."[1] In understanding the meaning of the Beatitudes and the word "blessed," it is defined here as "happy." Jesus wanted this large crowd of people to know how to be truly happy.

What makes you happy? Take a minute to think about it. Next, write down the things that make you happy. Get out a pen and use the space below to list these things. By each one, also write down why it makes you happy. How does each thing bring you happiness?

_____

_____

_____

1 "Did You Know?", *NIV Adventure Bible*, (Grand Rapids, MI: Zonderkidz, 2013), 1056.

What I love about the Beatitudes are that they start off saying "blessed are" and then list a type of person who is blessed (happy), followed by how they are blessed. There are eight Beatitudes listed in Matthew 5 and we are going to take a look at what each one means over the next eight days. We are going to find out eight different ways that Jesus says we can be truly happy (or blessed). Aren't you excited about that? I am! I can't wait to start tomorrow!

Holy God, we praise You for all things. Thank You for giving me Jesus to teach me the ways to be truly blessed and happy in this life. Open my heart to hear You speak to me each day. Amen.

Follow Me

Bring happiness to your teacher today at school. Draw a picture for them or leave a note on their desk telling them they are a great teacher and they are loved by Jesus.

30

Blessed Are the Poor in Spirit

Matthew 5:3

"Blessed are the poor in spirit, for theirs is the kingdom of heaven." Matthew 5:3

"We don't have any food in the house. We are so poor."

Those were the words my daughter uttered one day as she searched through the refrigerator and pantry for something to eat. I just shook my head as she said it, because there WAS stuff to eat in the house. It just wasn't any kind of food she liked or craved to eat at the moment. I immediately began to explain to her that she can't even begin to imagine what it's like to truly be poor and not have anything to eat.

Have those words ever come out of your mouth? I am sure they have at times when your parents didn't buy you something you wanted. Or when your parents told you they couldn't afford something. And maybe they were like me and had to explain to you what it really meant to be poor.

In this first Beatitude that Jesus talks about, He says that the poor in spirit are blessed because the kingdom of heaven is theirs. So what does that really mean? Do we really have to be poor to be able to live in the kingdom of heaven?

I believe Jesus wants us to know He sees the poor. He loves those who have nothing. He has not forgotten about them. He wants them to know they are blessed, and that His kingdom is theirs as well.

Jesus wants us not to forget about the poor. We aren't to turn our backs on those who are in need of something to eat or a place to sleep. He wants us to take care of those who are poor because they are His children, too. He wants us to share the things He has blessed us with, with those who have nothing.

What can you do to help those who are poor? Talk with your parents more about what your family can do for those in need.

Heavenly Father, thank You for all You have given me. Show me how to help others who are in need. Help me to serve them with the love You have shown me. Amen.

Follow Me

Call your local food bank. Ask them what items they currently need the most. Then go grocery shopping with your parents to buy these items and deliver them to the food bank.

Pumpkin Bread

3 cups sugar
1 cup vegetable oil
3 eggs
1 16oz. can pumpkin
3 cups flour
1 tsp. cloves

1 tsp. cinnamon
1 tsp. nutmeg
1 tsp. baking soda
½ tsp. salt
½ tsp. baking powder

Preheat oven to 350°. Beat sugar and oil in a bowl. Mix in eggs and pumpkin. Stir together flour, cloves, cinnamon, nutmeg, baking soda, salt, and baking powder in another bowl. Then sift that mixture. Stir flour mixture into pumpkin mixture in two additions. Divide batter equally into two loaf pans. Bake for 1 hour 10 minutes.

Something To Chew On

················

What is your favorite Bible verse?

31

Blessed Are Those Who Mourn

Matthew 5:4

"Blessed are those who mourn, for they will be comforted." Matthew 5:4

Can you think of a time in your life so far where you have truly mourned for something you lost? Maybe it was a family or friend who passed away, a pet who died, or your favorite toy that was very special to you. When you mourned those things, you cried. Tears, I'm sure, were flowing down your face and you were extremely sad.

In this Beatitude, Jesus wants us to know that those who mourn are blessed (or happy). How you can you be happy when you're sad? How can you be blessed when all you do is cry?

Jesus goes on to tell us that we are blessed when we are sad because we will be comforted. Your parents comfort you when you are sad. Your friends comfort you when you are sad. Your teachers comfort you when you are sad.

But did you know that when those people comfort you it's Jesus comforting you? In 2 Corinthians 1:3-4 it says, "Praise be to the God and Father of our Lord Jesus Christ, the Father of compassion and the God of all comfort, who comforts us in all our troubles, so that we can comfort those in any trouble with the comfort we ourselves receive from God."

Our God is a God of comfort. He comforts us in our sad times. And then what's really cool is that we can then use that same comfort He's given us and comfort someone else when they are sad.

We can be comforted by Him through reading the Bible. Any time you open God's Word, you can hear Him speak to you. The Bible is not an old book that doesn't mean anything. It's God's Word to us and it's alive today! So next time you are sad and God gives you a verse in the Bible to bring you comfort, you can use it to bring comfort to someone else when they are sad. Remember that you are blessed when you mourn because you will be comforted by our Lord and Savior, Jesus Christ.

God of Comfort, thank You for giving me comfort when I am sad. Help me to be a good friend and comfort others as You comfort me. In Jesus' name, Amen.

Follow Me

When you see someone who is crying or sad at school or at home, give them a hug. Tell them Jesus loves them and sees their sadness. Then share with them a Bible verse that brings you comfort in sad times.

Blessed Are the Meek
Matthew 5:5

"Blessed are the meek, for they will inherit the earth."
Matthew 5:5

Do you know someone who has a hard time listening, thinks they know it all, and is just a downright mean person?

A person like that is the complete opposite of someone who is meek. A meek person listens to God, obeys God and does what God asks of them. They are kind to everyone, and rarely speak a mean word. Wouldn't you rather be friends with someone who is meek? I know I would!

Jesus tells us in Matthew 5:5 that the meek are blessed (or happy) because they will inherit the earth. Hmm...what does it really mean to inherit the earth? Does that mean the earth will be ours?

If we look at Psalm 37:11 (yes, go grab your Bible and find this verse), it says, "But the meek will inherit the land and enjoy peace and prosperity." And I believe this to be true 100%! When you obey God and do all He asks of you, wouldn't you think that your life would be blessed? Yes, of course it would! You will be blessed and you will live at peace. You will find joy in everything you do, and you will be happy while you are here on this earth. That is the life of someone who inherits the earth.

How hard do you think it will be to be a person who is meek? Can you try to live your life obeying God and trusting Him in everything? I believe you can. I believe you must work hard at being a meek person, but I believe in you and I know you can do this.

Father God, I want to be meek. I want to listen to You and I want follow You with all my heart. Help me to live my life each day this way so I can live at peace with You. Amen.

Follow Me

Practice being meek today. Start your day asking God to help you listen and obey Him. Then listen throughout the day for God to tell you to do something. When you feel like He's talking to you, then do what He asks you to do, no matter how hard you think it will be.

Blessed Are the Hungry & Thirsty

Matthew 5:6

"Blessed are those who hunger and thirst for righteousness, for they will be filled." Matthew 5:6

When you think about being hungry and thirsty, you usually think about being hungry for some food to eat or being thirsty for something to drink. But, is that what Jesus is saying to us in Matthew 5:6?

The type of hunger and thirst He's talking about has nothing to do with food. It's a type of hunger and thirst that you really want as someone who follows the Lord. To be hungry and thirsty for righteousness means that you crave so much to be right with God. And to be right with God means you follow Him closely; you want nothing more than to get to know Him better. You can do this by spending time every morning with Him, reading His Word, praying, and listening for Him to speak to you. Being right with God also means obeying all He asks of you.

Jesus says that when you hunger and thirst for righteousness, you will be filled. Think about it this way, when you are hungry for food, what do you do? You eat something and you are no longer hungry, and you are satisfied. When you're thirsty for something to drink, what do you do? You drink something, your thirst is quenched or satisfied, and you are no longer dying of thirst. So when you are hungry and thirsty for God, what do you do? You do all you can to spend time with Him so you can get to know Him better and you will be filled and satisfied in Him.

In my life I go through times when I am really hungry and thirsty for God and to know Him better. Other times I don't work hard at having a good relationship with Him. I want to be hungry and thirsty all the time for God and His righteousness. I need to work hard at doing this every day. My prayer for you is that you will always want to be close to God and you will always hunger and thirst for Him. There's no better place to be then right next to the Lord.

Good God, help me to be hungry and thirsty to be close to You. Help me to spend time reading the Bible so I can know more about You and strive to be like You. I love You, Lord. Amen.

Follow Me

Spend five minutes today reading the Bible. Spend five or more minutes praying. And then spend another five minutes being silent and listening for God to speak to you.

Blessed Are the Merciful
Matthew 5:7

"Blessed are the merciful, for they will be shown mercy."
Matthew 5:7

Some of you may have never heard the word mercy before. To show mercy to someone means you show them forgiveness. You forgive them even when they don't deserve it. Jesus is saying to us here that those who are merciful will be shown mercy. Which means when we are forgiving to others, we will also be shown that same forgiveness.

Let's draw a picture here. In the first box, draw a picture of a person doing something that requires forgiveness. What has someone done to you where you have had to show forgiveness? In the second box, draw a picture of someone showing you forgiveness for something you did to them.

How hard was it to show mercy or forgiveness to your friend or family member who hurt you? I am sure it was a little difficult depending on what they did to you. But let's reverse the situation and imagine that you are the one who has hurt someone else. Aren't you hoping that they will show mercy to you and forgive you? Jesus tells us that when we show mercy to others, we will be shown mercy, not only by the friend that we hurt, but by Jesus Himself.

Now take your pen and write real big over the top of the two boxes above "Be Merciful." This will help remind you to always forgive, just as Jesus always forgives us.

Gracious Lord, forgive me when I hurt someone else. Help me to show mercy to others just as You show mercy all the time to me. In Jesus' name, Amen.

Follow Me

Today, if you do something that hurts someone, ask them for forgiveness. And if someone hurts you, and they ask you to forgive them, do it. Forgive as Jesus forgives.

Blessed Are the Pure in Heart

Matthew 5:8

"Blessed are the pure in heart, for they will see God."
Matthew 5:8

I want to see God! I want to see God! I want to see God!

I can picture you now. Your teacher has just asked you, "Who wants to see God?" Your first response might be, "Who wouldn't want to see God? I mean it's God. The God who created me and loves me. Yes, of course I want to see God!"

So you raise your hand, waving it back and forth rather excitedly. You might even be sitting on the edge of your seat, too. You are hoping she picks you because you really want to see God.

But then your teacher says something that catches you off guard and makes you put your hand down for a minute. She says you can see God, but you must have a pure heart. *A pure heart? What does that even mean?*

Having a pure heart means your heart is free of all evil things. It means you don't say mean things to people, or disobey your parents, or judge people by how they look, or spread gossip about someone you don't like. Having a pure heart is not easy, and something you will have to work hard at having, but the reward for having a pure heart is awesome…it means you will get to see God.

To see God here on this earth means being able to see Him in creation, in other people, in the things we do. We won't be able to physically see God with our eyes, but we will see Him through things He created. When we can see God, we will enjoy being with Him, we will be happy that He is our God, and we will do everything we can to be like Him.

Don't you want to live a life that allows you to see God? I know I do, and I will work hard at doing that every single day. So let's have pure hearts and keep them clean from all evil!

God of Love, thank You for allowing me to be on this earth. Help me to think about things before I do or say anything that might make my heart unclean. Give me a pure heart so that I can see You. In Jesus' name, Amen.

Follow Me

Write in the heart below ways you can have a pure heart (a heart that is clean, and free from wrongdoing). And then work every day at having a pure heart so you can see God.

Blessed Are the Peacemakers

Matthew 5:9

"Blessed are the peacemakers, for they will be called children of God." Matthew 5:9

If you ever step in my house in the mornings before school starts, you will hear a lot of yelling and fighting. That would be me trying to get my children up and out of the bed, making sure they have done all they need to do to be ready to go to school, and maybe even yelling at them to hurry up. It's not very peaceful at my house at that time of day.

I am sure there are times at your house when instead of being quiet and peaceful, it's loud and people are yelling. Maybe you are fighting with your brother or sister, maybe your parents are yelling at you to stop fighting, maybe your parents are yelling at you because you didn't do what they asked you to do. There are so many things which can cause our homes to be anything but peaceful.

Jesus says that we should all be at peace with one another. And in order to be at peace with others we must be peacemakers. Does a peacemaker create chaos? Does a peacemaker stir up conflict? No, a peacemaker does exactly what the word means…they live in peace with others. A peacemaker does everything they can to make sure everyone is not at odds with others. A peacemaker loves peace.

Jesus came to this world to bring us peace. And He accomplished just that! When we live at peace with one another we can live as children of God. And that means living our lives free from conflict or chaos.

Can I fill you in on a little secret? I'm a peacemaker. I love it when everyone is happy and gets along. I hate it when people fight. I want everyone to like each other and love each other. I want everyone to be at peace with each other.

Is my life always peaceful? Absolutely not. But I strive every day to make sure those living around me have peace with one another. Let's all be peacemakers! I believe the world would be a better place to live if we all were.

Prince of Peace, thank You for coming into this world and bringing us peace. Help us to find ways to live at peace with those around us. In Jesus' name, Amen.

Follow Me

Next time someone close to you—a cousin, a sister, a brother, or even your next door neighbor—does something to annoy you, choose not to start a fight with them. If you're an only child, then do this with a friend. Instead, kindly tell them to stop and then give them a hug. They might be so surprised by your kindness that they stop annoying you!

Ham Breakfast Rolls

3 Tbsp. mustard
3 Tbsp. poppy seeds
1 tsp. Worcestershire sauce
2 sticks butter

1 lb. shaved ham
½ lb. grated cheese
3 pkg. brown dinner rolls

Combine mustard, poppy seeds, Worcestershire sauce, and butter in a pot on the stovetop. Cook on low heat until mixture is melted. Cut dinner rolls in half lengthwise. Place bottom half of rolls on cookie sheet. Layer with ham and cheese. Spread mixture on top of rolls. Then put the other half of rolls on top. Bake at 400° for 15-20 minutes. Recipe can be cut in half if you want to make less.

Something To Chew On

· · · · · · · · · · · · · · · · · ·

**Would you rather write a letter to Jesus
or be able to talk to Jesus in person?**

Blessed Are Those Who Are Persecuted

Matthew 5:10

"Blessed are those who are persecuted because of
righteousness, for theirs is the kingdom of heaven."
Matthew 5:10

"Mom, my friend at school told me that God isn't real. And then he made fun of me for believing in God."

This was what my daughter said to me one day after school. She was sad, first of all, that her friend didn't go to church or believe that God was real. And second of all, that he made fun of her for her own belief in God. She didn't understand why he didn't believe or why he would make fun of her.

This is exactly what this Beatitude is talking about. Jesus says that everyone who believes in Him will not always be liked by everyone. There are people out there who don't believe He is real. They don't believe He died for our sins or that He rose again. They don't believe that Jesus is our Savior. And because they don't believe, they will give those who are Christians and who do believe in Jesus a hard time. There may be times in your life when you are made fun of because of your belief in Jesus.

But Jesus says not to give up. Don't let what others say make you feel bad or want to stop believing in Him. For those who are persecuted because of righteousness (which means being right with God or your belief in God), great is their reward. And what will that reward be? Your reward will be the kingdom of heaven. You will get to live in heaven forever with Jesus when you leave this earth. I can't think of any greater reward than this.

Remember that Jesus loves you. Remember that He is real. Remember to be strong in your faith and continue to believe in Him no matter what anyone else says. Why? Because your reward is the kingdom of heaven.

Loving God, help me to continue to show Your love to all people, even if they make fun of me for believing in You. Help me to be strong in my faith and to continue living my life for You. In Jesus' name, Amen.

Follow Me

Take your Bible to school today. Share your favorite verse with your teacher or with a friend.

38

Love Your Enemies
Luke 6:27-36

"But to you who are listening I say: Love your enemies, do good to those who hate you, bless those who curse you, pray for those who mistreat you." Luke 6:27-28

You want me to do what, Lord?

That might be the response you first give when you hear that Jesus asks us to love our enemies. You aren't too thrilled to hear that because there are some people at school who are mean to you. They make fun of you and call you names. There also may be some people at school who don't include you in their conversations at lunch or don't ask you to play with them at recess. They intentionally leave you out and you don't like them. These aren't the kind of people you want to love.

But let's look at how Jesus loved. Did He choose only certain people to love? Did He only love the people that believed in Him? No, He loved everybody. He came to save each and every person on this earth because we are all children of God. And He asks us to love everyone, even those people we really don't like.

Is that going to be hard? Yes of course! But because something is hard doesn't mean that we shouldn't do it.

Look at the Scripture verse above from Luke 6:27-28. Jesus says that we should love our enemies and the way we do that is by doing good to those people who hate us. It's saying a blessing over the people who don't like you. And the best thing we can do for those people who don't like us or those that we don't like, is to pray for them.

What do we pray for them? You pray that God will help you see them as He does. It's only then that we will be able to love them. We need to see as Jesus sees them, as His children who are loved by Him.

Heavenly Father, You know I'm having a hard time loving someone right now. It's hard to forgive them when they have done something mean to me. But I ask right now that You help me see that person as You see them. Help me to be kind to them even when they aren't kind to me. Help me to love them as You love them. In Jesus' name, Amen.

Follow Me

Write down the people who you find a hard time loving right now. And then pray for them.

Jesus Teaches Prayer

Luke 11:1–4

"Lord, teach us to pray, just as John taught his disciples."
Luke 11:1b

I don't know how to pray.

Have you ever said those words? There may be times when you feel like you don't know what to say to God. Maybe because you feel like your prayers aren't being answered or perhaps because you feel you aren't important enough to pray to God. Or maybe because you feel there is a certain way to pray and you don't know how.

I think the disciples felt just like you do. They observed Jesus praying many times. Perhaps they wanted to know how to pray just as Jesus prayed since He was the Son of God. I believe they desired to be like Him and to pray just like Him.

Jesus taught them what we call today "The Lord's Prayer." He gave them (and us) an example of how to pray. Those parts include: praising God, asking God to provide for our daily needs, forgiving us of our sins, keeping us from temptation of things we should not do or things we do not need, and rescuing us from the evil one, which is the devil.

What I want you to remember, though, is there aren't certain words you have to use or say in order for God to hear you. He actually says this in Matthew 6:7, "And when you pray, do not keep on babbling like pagans, for they think they will be heard because of their many words."

Apparently, some people thought they had to use big, fancy words in order for God to hear their prayers. Not so says Jesus. No big words needed.

So when you pray, don't think you have to pray in a certain way. Pray because you want to talk to God. Pray, believing with all your heart He will answer you. Pray, knowing that He does hear you. And if you are at a loss for words, pray using the example Jesus gave us in the Lord's Prayer.

Father God, thank You for teaching me how to pray. Thank You for hearing me and for listening to me. Help me to always follow You. In Jesus' name, Amen.

Follow Me

This may be a bold move for you, but what if you prayed before your lunch at school? And not just pray to yourself, but what if you prayed with the friends at your table? Try doing this and see how it goes. You might just help someone come to know Jesus through your lunch prayers.

Do Not Worry

Matthew 6:25-34

"Therefore do not worry about tomorrow, for tomorrow will worry about itself. Each day has enough trouble of its own." Matthew 6:34

What do you worry about? Take a second to write these things down below:

When I was your age, I found myself worrying about many things…making friends, taking tests at school, making good grades, getting sick, doing well in my sports games, and I also worried about dogs biting me (I was terrified of dogs). That seems like a lot for one kid to worry about it!

But do you want to know something, though? Jesus says we have no need to worry. That's right…Jesus says that in the Bible.

In Matthew chapter 6, Jesus is speaking to the Jewish people. He knows their hearts and He knows exactly what they need to hear. I am assuming that Jewish people were worriers, just like me and you. By what Jesus says I am assuming they worried about finding enough food to eat and water to drink. He also mentioned clothing so I assume they wondered if they would have enough clothes to wear. Jesus reassures them they need not worry. He reminds them if He provides food for the birds to eat and clothes the earth with beautiful lilies and grass, then won't He provide so much more for His people?

So what can you do if you worry about things? You can turn those worries into prayers. Ask Jesus to help you be free of those worries. Ask Him to put your mind at ease and give you peace. Jesus doesn't tell us to worry. He tells us to be free from worry. And I believe you can do that when you take all your worries to Him in prayer.

Prince of Peace, forgive me when I worry. Help me find peace during the times when I worry. Remind me every day of how You provide for me. Help me to trust in You. In Jesus' name, Amen.

Follow Me

When I feel worried, I carry a cross in my pocket. It helps me feel Jesus' presence in worrisome times. All I have to do is reach in my pocket and be reminded that Jesus is with me and there is nothing to worry about. If you don't have a pocket cross, ask your parents to go online and buy one for you.

The Golden Rule

Matthew 7:12

"So in everything, do to others what you would have them do to you, for this sums up the Law and the Prophets." Matthew 7:12

I turned on the vacuum and began vacuuming the living room like my mom told me to do. Secretly, I was happy to do this because I knew it would scare my little sister so much. You see, she was terrified of vacuum cleaners. Not sure why, but maybe it was because they were so loud or maybe because she was afraid of getting sucked up into it. No matter what the reason, she extremely disliked vacuum cleaners.

She was sitting on the sofa watching that vacuum cleaner draw closer to her. As I began to vacuum, I decided I would have a little fun. I kept the vacuum on and lifted it up and put it near her face. She began screaming hysterically and I couldn't stop laughing. And of course, I got in trouble for this.

Was I following the Golden Rule when I was scaring my sister with the vacuum cleaner? Absolutely not.

The Golden Rule is what Jesus says in Matthew 7:12: "Do to others what you would have them do to you." Basically, we should treat others the way we want to be treated. That means doing things to others or saying things to others because we would want to be treated the same way.

What if the roles were reversed in my situation above? Do you think I would want my sister to treat me the way I treated her? Of course not. I would not want someone to take my fear and literally put it in my face. I was definitely not treating her the way I would want to be treated.

The next time you do something to hurt someone, take time to think about the Golden Rule. Ask yourself, "Would I want to be treated this way?" And if your answer is no, then don't do it. Or if you've already done it, ask that person for forgiveness.

Try your best to follow the Golden Rule. Be kind and treat others the way you want to be treated.

Loving God, thank You for giving us the Golden Rule. Thank You for teaching me about showing kindness to everyone. Forgive me when I mess up and don't treat others the way I want to be treated. Show me the way to love others as You love me. In Jesus' name, Amen.

Follow Me

I am sure you want to be treated with kindness and respect. So today, practice kindness. Go out of your way to be kind, even to the people who are not kind to you.

Building on the Rock
Matthew 7:24-29

"Therefore everyone who hears these words of mine and puts them into practice is like a wise man who built his house on the rock." Matthew 7:24

Let's take a poll…

If you wanted to build a house, would you prefer it to be built on sand or would you prefer it to be built on rock?

Now, before you vote, let's think about this. What happens to things that are built on sand? They wash away very easily, right? (Think about all those sandcastles you worked hard to build on the beach).

What happens to things that are built on rock? They are strong and they hold up. They are not going to fall. So I think it's safe to assume that you would cast your vote for building your house on the rock.

In Matthew 7, Jesus tells this parable (a story) to some people. He says in verse 24 that if we hear His Word (which is the Bible) and we do what it says, that our lives will be strong just like a house built on rock. But in verse 26, He says that if we read His Word and hear it but do not do what it says that our lives will crumble easily just like a house built on sand.

So what is Jesus really trying to say here?

He's telling us to make sure we build our lives around Him. In order to stay strong and be solid in our faith, we need to be reading the Bible, listening to Jesus, doing what He says to do, praying, going to church, and telling others about Him. If we do these things our faith in Jesus will never fall. It will stay strong forever.

There will be times in your life when you don't stay on the rock, but just remember that Jesus is always with you and He will help you get back on the rock and will keep you strong.

Father God, I praise You for who you are. I thank You for giving me a rock to stand on. Thank You for showing me how to live my life. Keep me strong in my faith and help me to always trust in You. In Jesus' name, Amen.

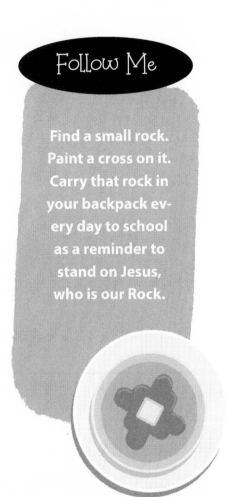

Follow Me

Find a small rock. Paint a cross on it. Carry that rock in your backpack every day to school as a reminder to stand on Jesus, who is our Rock.

Cream Cheese Banana Bread

¾ cup butter, softened
1 8oz. pkg cream cheese,
  softened
2 cups sugar
2 large eggs
3 cups all-purpose flour

½ tsp. baking powder
½ tsp. baking soda
½ tsp. salt
4 medium bananas, mashed
½ tsp. vanilla extract

Beat butter and cream cheese with electric mixer until creamy. Gradually add sugar, beating until light and fluffy. Add eggs (one at a time, beating until well blended).

Combine flour, baking powder, baking soda, and salt in a separate bowl. Gradually add to butter mixture until well blended. Stir in bananas and vanilla extract. Divide batter equally and pour into two greased and floured 8x4" loaf pans.

Bake at 350° for one hour or until toothpick comes out clean. If you notice the top getting too brown you can put aluminum foil over it for the last 15 minutes. Cool for 10 minutes before removing from the pan. Allow bread to cool for 30 minutes before slicing and serving.

Something To Chew On

· · · · · · · · · · · · · · · · · · ·

**What is something you have done that
you need to ask Jesus to forgive you?**

Judging Others
Luke 6:37a

"Do not judge, and you will not be judged." Luke 6:37a

What does it mean to judge someone? Are we like a courtroom judge who sits high up on their bench and sentences people? Or can we judge people in our hearts right where we are today?

I think you know the answer to this one.

We judge people without even realizing we judge them, each and every day. Judging means that we criticize someone for something they did or said or even because of how they look. Take a look around at the people in your class at school, or at your family sitting around the dinner table. I am sure you have thought things in your mind about how they dress or how their hair is fixed or the way they act. You might even say these thoughts out loud at times.

Have you ever stopped to think about how the way we judge people affects them? The words we say and the way we look down upon others can be so hurtful. It can truly harm one's self-esteem and make them feel bad about themselves.

I like to compare judging others and using words that are hurtful to a tube of toothpaste. When you squeeze the toothpaste out, can you get it back in? Try it and see what happens. It's rather difficult to put toothpaste back into the tube once it has come out.

The same goes for the words that we say when we judge others. We can't take those words back. We can't put them back into our mouths and forget we ever said them. They are out and we can't put them back in.

Imagine the tables being turned and you are the one who is receiving the judgement and hurtful words. It's not much fun, is it? Jesus says we are not to judge so that we won't be judged.

Jesus also tells us to treat others the way we want to be treated. So the next time you want to say something mean about someone, remember that Jesus tells us not to judge others. And then ask Jesus to help you see others the way He sees them. When we can see people as He does, this will help transform our thoughts into good ones and we will love others the way He does.

God of All, help me to remember that I am not to judge other people. Open my eyes so I can see others the way You see them. In Jesus' name, Amen.

Follow Me

The next time you think or say something as a way of judging another person, do a random act of kindness for them. That could be something as simple as a smile, or even asking them to play with you at recess.

Forgiveness
Luke 6:37b

"Forgive, and you will be forgiven." Luke 6:37b

She called me chubby and said I need to exercise more. That was so mean and I'll never forgive her!

Those were words spoken to a child one day when she was in elementary school. The words stung and cut straight to her heart. She didn't understand why someone she knew and considered a friend would have said such harsh words. She had no intention of forgiving that friend. They didn't deserve it. She was ready to let that be the end of their friendship.

Have you ever felt the pain much like this child experienced? Maybe a friend at school made fun of you. Maybe it was a sibling who cut you with their words. Or perhaps, even in the heat of the moment, what your parent said hurt deeply. Did you forgive them or did you let their words create bitterness in your heart?

I'll be honest and tell you that forgiveness is hard. There are some days when I don't want to forgive someone for what they did or said. They don't deserve my forgiveness. I would rather remain angry at them forever than forgive them or be nice to them again.

But is that what Jesus would do?

No, Jesus would do none of that. Jesus tells us to forgive. He says in Luke 6:37b, "Forgive, and you will be forgiven." Part of being forgiven for what we do requires us to forgive others their wrongs towards us. And why should we have to forgive? Because Jesus forgives us. Wouldn't it be sad if Jesus didn't forgive us? But we don't have to worry about that because we know that He does. All we need to do is accept Him as our Savior, believe He died for our sins, and confess our sins to Him and He says we will be forgiven. Isn't that amazing!

We are not only called to seek forgiveness from God and those we hurt, but we are also called to forgive others as Jesus does us. I hope you will work hard each day at forgiving the people who have caused you harm. Follow the example of Christ and forgive others. And remember He has forgiven you, too.

Forgiving God, thank You for teaching me about forgiveness. Thank You for showing me how to forgive. Help me to have a heart like Yours and forgive others as You forgive me. In Jesus' name, Amen.

Follow Me

Make a list of people whom you need to forgive. Pray and ask God to help you forgive them. After you pray, take a red marker and mark through their name. On the other side of that, write FORGIVEN by their name. That will be a helpful reminder to you that God forgives them and that you forgive them, too.

Give to Others
Luke 6:38

"Give, and it will be given to you. A good measure,
pressed down, shaken together and running over, will
be poured into your lap. For with the measure you use, it
will be measured to you." Luke 6:38

Isn't it so much fun to get presents? Don't you just love ripping the wrapping paper off the present and tearing into the box? Excitement builds and builds and you can't wait to see what's inside. Maybe it's that thing you asked your parents to get you. Or maybe it's a total surprise. No matter what it is, you just love getting presents.

Now, let's reverse that situation. How do you feel when you give a gift to someone else? Do you find yourself getting just as excited as you do when you get one? Or do you really wish you were the one opening that gift?

Let me share with you that giving to others brings more joy to me than getting gifts myself. There's just something about watching the face of the person opening the gift that makes my heart do a happy dance. I love to watch their face light up as they open it. I love to see their reaction.

And you want to know what's even more fun? Giving a gift without the receiver knowing that it was you who gave it. Sometimes I like to give anonymously, especially if it's a gift for someone who is really in need. I want them to see it as a gift from God instead of a gift from me.

Jesus says that if we give, it will be given to us. Do you understand what that really means? When we give to others, God will give back to us. Or when we give to God, God will give back to us. I have been on the receiving end of a gift plenty of times in my life. Sometimes it's been when I am in need and I am always so blessed by watching God work. I love to give to others because I have been blessed so much by what others have given to me.

But most importantly, I give to God because He gave His one and only Son for me. Jesus gave up His own life so I could live forever with Him in heaven one day. Talk about the greatest of all gifts. And God did this because He loves us so very much. I pray you will have a heart for giving to others just as God gave to you.

Giving God, thank You for the gift of Jesus. Help me to have a heart for giving to others just as You gave to me. I love You, Lord. In Jesus' name, Amen.

Follow Me

If you get an allowance, use it to buy a gift for someone else. Maybe for a friend who is in need of something they cannot afford. Or use it to buy something for your sibling. And if you so choose, give it without them knowing it was from you. Then just sit back and watch the joy spread over their face as they receive that gift.

The Parable of the Sower
Luke 8:1-15

"But the seed on good soil stands for those with a noble and good heart, who hear the word, retain it, and by persevering produce a crop." Luke 8:15

Jesus loved to teach people by using parables (stories that give a meaning). Sometimes Jesus doesn't explain what the parable means, but in this parable He does.

The Parable of the Sower talks about a farmer who planted seeds on four different types of soil. The first seeds he sowed were on the path. They got walked all over and the birds ate them up. Jesus goes on to explain that the seeds in this story represent the Word of God. The seeds on the path are meant to represent people who hear the word of God, but the devil comes and takes the words away and they no longer believe (Luke 8:11-12).

Some seeds fell on rocky ground and when they came up they withered because they didn't have any moisture (Luke 8:6). Jesus said this represents the people who hear the Word of God and are very happy and joyful when they hear it, but they have no root. They believe it for a little while, but when times get hard they give up and walk away from God (Luke 8:13).

Other seeds fell on thorns. The seeds grew but they also had thorns grow up with them. The thorns eventually choked the plant (Luke 8:7). Jesus said this represents people who hear the Word of God and accept it, but they are so caught up in life's worries, in being rich and having it all, that they do not mature in their faith (Luke 8:14).

The last seeds fell on good soil. When the plants came up, they produced a good crop, more than what was actually sown (Luke 8:8). Jesus said this represents those people who do the right thing, have good hearts, who hear the Word of God, commit it to memory and live by it. These seeds produce a good crop (Luke 8:15).

I want to be like the seeds sown on good soil. I want to always do what God wants me to do. I want to always follow the Lord no matter what happens. I want to read my Bible and learn it, being able to recall Scripture when I need it. And I want to live out God's Word in my daily life. Will you join me? Let's be good seeds in this world!

Almighty God, help me to be a good seed. Help me to commit to You in all ways and to live my life as an example of You. In Jesus' name, Amen.

Follow Me

Plant your favorite seeds today...a flower, fruit, or vegetable. Take care of it and water it daily. Watch your plant grow. When it is ready, give that plant to someone or give your fruits or vegetables away to others.

Be the Light
Luke 8:16–18

"No one lights a lamp and hides it in a clay jar or puts it under a bed. Instead, they put it on a stand, so that those who come in can see the light." Luke 8:16

Experiment time! Grab a parent, as this will be something you will need their help with. You'll also need a candle, a lighter, and a glass.

Light the candle. Watch it glow brightly. Now put the glass over the top of the candle and cover it up. What happens to the candle?

As you saw, the candle goes out. No more flame. There is not enough oxygen inside the glass to keep it shining. The lack of oxygen makes the flame extinguish. No more light.

In this passage in Luke chapter 8, Jesus is talking about His light that shines through us. When we come to know Jesus and have a passion and love for Him, that love will shine brightly through us. It will be hard to contain such a strong light. We will not want to hide His light under a jar or put it under a bed, we will want to share it with others.

Have you ever sung the song "This Little Light of Mine?" Each verse says:

This little light of mine, I'm gonna let it shine!

Hide it under a bushel? NO! I'm gonna let it shine!

Won't let Satan blow it out, I'm gonna let it shine!

We aren't to hide it or let Satan blow it out. We are to let the light of Jesus shine through us.

Light of the World, thank You for all You do for me. Help me to be a light for You in my city. Give me courage to tell others about You. May my light shine brightly for You, Jesus. In Your name we pray, Amen.

Follow Me

With your parents, light a candle. Hold it up and pray, asking Jesus to help you be His light in this world.

Jesus Calms the Storm

Mark 4:35-41

"He said to his disciples, 'Why are you so afraid? Do you still have no faith?'" Mark 4:40

Imagine this scene.

You've had a long day. Lots of walking, talking to people, and learning from your Teacher. Then your Teacher tells you to get into the boat. It's late in the evening as you climb aboard. You start to feel a breeze pick up as you sail across to the other side. But then things become a little scary. That breeze turns into a great windstorm. Everyone on board is afraid.

Then you remember your Teacher, the One who is able to perform miracles. Surely He will be able to help you. So you go in search for Him only to find Him asleep. Who sleeps through a storm?

You wake Him up and He does something you have not seen anyone do before. He says "Peace! Be still!" All of a sudden the wind dies down and is calm. How can this be that even the wind and the waves obey Him? Then He asks you a question that makes you think hard. He says, "Why are you so afraid? Do you still have no faith?"

This scene is what happened the night the disciples and Jesus were in a boat. The Teacher is Jesus. What would your answer be if He asked you that question?

There are things in this world that scare us. Many things, actually. And while it's hard to let go of some of the things that we are afraid of, there is one person we can give those fears to, and that is Jesus. He asks us to let go and have faith. He will take care of us and He will always be with us.

Remember to have faith in Jesus and trust Him. Give Him your fears and allow Him to crush them for you. Listen to Him say "Peace! Be still!", and then let go of your fears.

Almighty God, thank You for taking away my fears. Help me to remember to have faith and trust in You. Help me to remember that You are always with me. In Jesus' name, Amen.

Follow Me

The next time you feel afraid, get out some paper and write down what you are afraid of. As a way of giving your fears to Jesus, draw a big cross over each fear and say a prayer. Give those fears to Jesus and remember He is with you.

Cinnamon Toast

2-3 slices of bread
Butter
Sugar
Cinnamon

Place 2-3 slices of bread on a cookie sheet. Spread butter on them (squeeze butter works the best). Next, sprinkle with sugar then cinnamon (put on as much as you like or as much as your parents say is good). Put in oven at 350°. Cook till bottom of bread is lightly toasted.

Something To Chew On

· · · · · · · · · · · · · · ·

If Jesus was coming for breakfast at your house today, what type of dishes would you serve food on?

The Pool of Healing
John 5:1-9

"Then Jesus said to him, 'Get up! Pick up your mat and walk.'" John 5:8

If you walked into a hospital, what would you find? You would find doctors and nurses, but mostly you would find a building full of sick people -- those in need of healing--people who want to be made well.

In the Bible story today, we find people who are in need of heal-ing, but they aren't hanging out in a hospital. These people are dis-abled (lame, paralyzed and blind) and they are sitting by a pool. Seems odd, right? Why would someone who wants to be well be sitting next to a pool?

Back then, it was believed that an angel would come to stir the waters and when it did, those who were able to get in the pool would be healed. But sometimes those who are disabled aren't able to get somewhere unless someone helps them.

That's what happened to the man in our story today. When Jesus asked him if he wanted to get well, the man thought that Jesus was saying that he needed to get into the pool to be healed because his response to Jesus' question was that there was no one to help him into the pool (he couldn't walk).

But Jesus wasn't going to use the pool to heal this man, was He? No, He was going to heal him by just speaking the word. We see in verse 8 what Jesus says, "Get up! Pick up your mat and walk." And instantly this man was healed! He got up, took up the mat he was sitting on and walked. It was a miracle of healing!

I love this story because we see the power Jesus has over sickness. We see that all He has to do is speak a word over any type of illness or sickness and we can be made well.

But sometimes, healing doesn't happen instantly. Sometimes it may take days or weeks or even years for people to be healed. No matter how long it takes for you to overcome an illness, remember that Jesus is with you. He walks beside you and gives you the strength and power to get through it. Don't give up hope if you aren't healed instantly like the man in this story. Just continue to believe in Jesus' healing power and in His love for you.

Powerful God, thank You for bringing healing to me when I am sick. Help me to always trust in You even when healing doesn't come when I want it to. In Jesus' name, Amen.

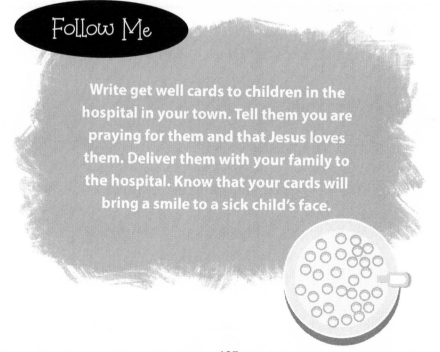

Follow Me

Write get well cards to children in the hospital in your town. Tell them you are praying for them and that Jesus loves them. Deliver them with your family to the hospital. Know that your cards will bring a smile to a sick child's face.

The Workers Are Few

Matthew 9:25-28

"Then he said to his disciples, 'The harvest is plentiful but the workers are few.'" Matthew 9:37

Have you ever been asked by your parents to do a chore at your house that seemed impossible? It was such a big chore that you didn't know how you would ever be able to get it all done. How did this make you feel? Overwhelmed when you saw all the work you had to do? Or maybe you felt ready to tackle this big chore?

In Matthew 9, we find Jesus doing the one thing God asked Him to do: sharing His love with everyone. Jesus was going through all the towns teaching about God, even healing sicknesses and diseases. So many people were coming to Him in need of healing, but also just wanting to listen to His teaching. Lots and lots of people sought Jesus out.

Do you think Jesus became overwhelmed when God asked Him to spread His love to everyone? No, just the opposite. He had compassion on them and never stopped teaching and loving people.

Jesus then tells His disciples that He needs their help in sharing about God. But He tells them "the harvest is plentiful but the workers are few." (Matthew 9:37). This means there are so many people in this world that need to hear about Him. However, the number of people who are willing to share His love are few.

As Christians, we are called to share the love of God with everyone. Jesus needs us to talk to other people about Him. He needs us to be kind, to love others, to be brave and speak His name to all people. Can you do that? I believe you can! Jesus needs you. Go out today and be one of God's workers!

Loving God, I know there are many people in the world who need to hear about You. Show me today who I can share Your love with. Help me to be brave and share Your name with everyone. In Jesus' name, Amen.

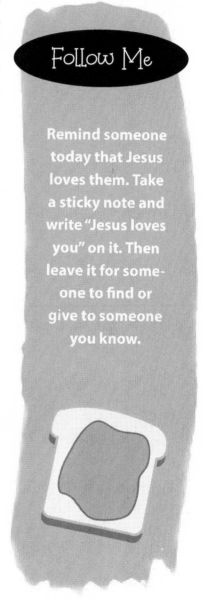

Follow Me

Remind someone today that Jesus loves them. Take a sticky note and write "Jesus loves you" on it. Then leave it for someone to find or give to someone you know.

51

Jesus Feeds 5,000 People

John 6:1-15

"When they had all had enough to eat, he said to his disciples, 'Gather the pieces that are left over. Let nothing be wasted.' So they gathered them and filled twelve baskets with the pieces of the five barley loaves left over by those who had eaten." John 6:12

Mom, I am so hungry! I need food!

Ever said that to your mother before? I believe we have all been so hungry at times that we thought we would die. It's not much fun when your stomach is growling and you can't find any food.

I can only imagine that's how the people who followed Jesus felt the day they followed Him to the other side of the Sea of Galilee. They loved hearing Him teach and preach. They wanted to go where He went so they could learn more from Him and see more miracles He would do.

But when it came time for dinner, the disciples were ready to send everyone away because they needed to get their own food. Do you think Jesus wanted that? No. This was an opportune time to perform yet another miracle and to show the people who He was so they could believe in Him even more.

The disciples weren't sure what Jesus' plan was. They had only managed to find five barley loaves of bread and two small fish from a boy in the crowd. How was Jesus going to feed the 5,000 men (not even counting the women and children) with such little food?

But Jesus knew what He was doing. He took the fish and bread, gave thanks, and distributed it to everyone. The food had multiplied and there were even leftovers! Twelve baskets of leftovers to be exact. Everyone was amazed!

On that day Jesus provided the food needed to feed 5,000+ people. And He continues to provide the same for all of us today. He provides food we need to survive. He provides water for us to drink to keep us hydrated. He provides all we need at the exact moment when we need it. He may not provide for us in the way we want Him to provide, but He definitely gives us what we need when we need it. Thank You, God, for providing for us!

Gracious God, thank You for giving me what I need. Thank You for giving me enough to live on. Help me to always be grateful for the ways You provide for me. In Jesus' name, Amen.

Follow Me

There may be people at your lunch table who do not bring much food from home. Share some of your lunch with someone at school who needs more to eat.

Jesus Walks on Water
Matthew 14:22-23

"But Jesus immediately said to them: 'Take courage! It is I. Don't be afraid.'" Matthew 14:27

Have you ever seen those little bugs in rivers or lakes that sit on top of the water? You know…the ones that seem to glide across the water without ever sinking?

Those little insects are what I like to call Jesus bugs. I call them that because they walk on the water. They remind me of the story of the time Jesus did yet another miracle. It was something no one else could do.

Jesus had just finished feeding the 5,000 people. He was tired, but He wanted to go up to the mountain by Himself to pray. So He put His disciples in the boat and told them He would catch up with them on the other side. And then He went to pray.

Later that night Jesus was ready to meet back up with His disciples. They were still out on the lake, so how do you think He got to them? He didn't take another boat to get to them. He didn't get a jet ski. He didn't swim to them. He walked to them…on top of the water.

How would you react if you saw Jesus walking toward you on the water? I have a feeling you would be a little freaked out much like the disciples were. They were so afraid because they thought Jesus was a ghost! But when Peter realized it was Jesus, he asked Jesus if he could come to Him on the water. Jesus said for him to come. And Peter began walking on water, too!

But once Peter realized what he was doing, he began to sink. And Jesus had to save him. Jesus asked Peter, "You of little faith, why did you doubt?" (Matthew 14:31).

Have you ever doubted Jesus? Have you ever felt that something was so impossible that even Jesus could not do it? Did you ever doubt Jesus because you didn't believe He would hear you or listen to you?

Doubt is something that creeps into our minds a lot. You may find that you stop praying for something because you doubt that Jesus will answer your prayer. Why bother, right?

Kids, you don't need to doubt Jesus. He hears your prayers. He loves you. He is with you. He may not answer your prayer in the way you want, but He will answer you because He cares for you. Don't let doubt take over your mind and keep you from having faith in Jesus. Stand strong and firm in your faith. And keep praying!

Mighty God, help me to have a strong faith in You. Help me to never doubt and to always believe in You and Your unfailing love. Give me strength to persevere and never doubt You. In Jesus' name, Amen.

Follow Me

Find a notebook and write down your prayer requests. And then pray those every day. When God answers, go back and write down how He answered your prayer. You will be amazed!

Bread of Life

John 6:35

"Then Jesus declared, 'I am the bread of life. Whoever comes to me will never go hungry, and whoever believes in me will never be thirsty.'" John 6:35

Do you want to know something about me?

I love bread! I could eat bread with every meal and even for snacks. I love sub bread, crescent rolls, Hawaiian bread, pumpkin bread, banana bread, onion rolls (great for sandwiches), but I think my favorite bread of all is a croissant. Those are so yummy! (I have a friend who owns her own bakery and she makes the best croissants!). Bread is so good!

In our Bible story today, we see that Jesus calls Himself the bread of life. Is He really saying that He is bread? Sounds a little confusing, right?

But Jesus doesn't literally mean that He is bread. He is saying to His followers that He is all they need to live spiritually. When we accept Jesus and believe in Him, we are given eternal life. He is the bread that can help us live forever. He is all we need in order to have everlasting life with God.

Remember the story of the Israelites when Moses helped them be free from Pharaoh in Egypt? They wandered in the wilderness for forty years. What did God provide for them every day? Manna… which is bread! He gave them bread to eat so they wouldn't be hungry and could live. But now God sent His Son to be our bread of life today. He came into this world to save us and show us the way to live forever.

Look back at our verse above from John 6:35. Jesus said that whoever comes to Him and believes in Him will never be hungry or thirsty. Why? Because He is our bread of life. No matter what happens in your life, it's always important to believe in Jesus and remember that He is with you. Remember that Jesus is your bread of eternal life!

Bread of Life, thank You for saving me so that I can live with You forever. Help me to remember that You never leave me and are always with me. I love You, Lord. Amen.

Follow Me

Bake your favorite bread today (with the help of your parents). Give it to someone to remind them that Jesus is the bread of life.

Hard Teaching

John 6:60-69

"From this time many of his disciples turned back and no longer followed him." John 6:66

When you are at school, is there ever a time when you get so frustrated because you cannot understand what the teacher is trying to teach you? For me, it was having to do math in my head. There was a time in 4th grade when we were learning how to give back the correct change without using a calculator. The teacher made each of us get up in front of the class to do this. She would tell us what something cost, tell us the amount of money they gave to pay for it, and then we were to give her back the correct amount of change. I hated doing this so much because I could not do it! It was extremely hard for me to do math in my head (and it still is today). I remember getting so frustrated and pretty much gave up trying to learn it.

That's exactly what happened with some of the disciples in our story today. They found the teachings of Jesus too hard. Verse 60 says, "On hearing it, many of his disciples said, 'This is a hard teaching. Who can accept it?'" They were frustrated by all that Jesus was teaching. How could anyone believe and follow Jesus exactly as He said? It seemed impossible to them!

So those disciples gave up. They threw in the towel and said, "Forget it…we aren't following Jesus." Now, I just want to point out that in the verse above the disciples it talks about were not the twelve disciples that Jesus called to follow Him. The people who followed and believed in Him were also called disciples. The twelve disciples didn't give up. They believed in Jesus and did everything they could to follow Him.

Following Jesus is hard. There will be times when we are called to be different than others. There will be times when we have to do the right thing, even when our friends do something else. It will be difficult to do, but that is when we must have a strong faith in Jesus and trust in Him. I urge you not to give up as some of the followers of Jesus did. I pray you will choose to walk closely with Jesus even when times are tough.

I believe in you. I know you can do it. Don't give up when following Jesus gets too hard.

Lord, I find it so hard to follow You at times. Help me not to give up when following You means going against what others are doing. Help me to be brave and to stand up for You and follow You always. In Jesus' name, Amen.

Follow Me

If you don't already have one, go buy a W.W.J.D. bracelet. (You can buy these on Amazon). This stands for "What would Jesus do." Wear that bracelet as a reminder to follow the ways of Jesus. When you are faced with a decision of what to do, pray and ask Jesus what He would do.

Butter Top Coffee Cake

(an old favorite recipe from Cairo, Illinois)

Coffee Cake Dough

1 package yeast	2 eggs
¼ cup warm water	1 tsp. salt
1 cup milk	½ cup sugar
¼ cup shortening	4-5 cups flour

Dissolve yeast in warm water. Scald milk and melt shortening in hot milk. Cool. Beat eggs. Add salt and sugar and mix. Add milk and shortening and mix. Add yeast and mix. Using a mixer, mix flour into batter a cup at a time. Cover with wax paper and let rise two hours or overnight. When dough has doubled, put it on a floured cloth on a board and knead 200 strokes. This makes enough dough for 4 coffee cakes. Divide the dough. Roll dough to fit two 9x13" pans. Put coffee cake topping on dough (see recipe below) and let it sit in a warm place for two hours. Bake 15-20 minutes at 350° on middle shelf.

Coffee Cake Topping

¾ cup butter	¼ cup powdered milk
1 ½ cups sugar	2 Tbsp. flour
2 eggs	1 tsp. vanilla

Cream butter till light and fluffy. Add sugar as you continue beating. Add eggs, one at a time. Add powdered milk, flour and vanilla. Beat some more. The topping should be very light and fluffy. Spread topping on dough and follow directions above.

Something To Chew On

· · · · · · · · · · · · · · · · · ·

What do you want to praise the Lord for today?

Dazzling White

Luke 9:28–36

*"As he was praying, the appearance of his face changed,
and his clothes became as bright as a flash of lightning."*
Luke 9:29

Have you ever bought a new pair of white tennis shoes, or a pair of white shorts, or even a nice white shirt? You really love them because they are so clean and bright. Your parents love that they are clean and bright, too! But let's be real for a second…they don't stay that way, do they? They are transformed into a dingy color that is anything but bright and clean. That's what happens when you play hard outside and get dirt on them, right?

One day three of the disciples saw Jesus wearing some really clean, bright clothes and they were amazed at what they saw. Jesus had taken Peter, James, and John up on a mountain to pray. Then something happened to Jesus while they were all praying…something they had never seen before in their lives. Jesus' face began to change and His clothes began to shine super bright. They were sparkling white and no one had ever seen something so bright before.

The Bible calls this Jesus' Transfiguration. That's a big word that means changing into something that's more beautiful. Jesus was definitely changing right before their eyes.

We will never be able to see something like this happen, but we can definitely take a look at ourselves to see if we could change into something more beautiful. And I'm not talking about your physical appearance. You don't need to change your hair, or change your clothes, or look different on the outside. I'm talking about a change that can happen on the inside.

When we accept Jesus as our Savior, we begin to change into something more beautiful on the inside. We will want to be a better person and live more like Him. We will try hard at changing our attitude and be more positive than negative. We will try hard to say kind words to others instead of hateful ones. We will try hard every day to be like Jesus.

Will we always be perfect? Absolutely not. Will we mess up? Yes, of course! But because of Jesus we are given forgiveness for messing up and we get to try again every day.

Take a look at yourself today. What can you do to change and be more beautiful on the inside?

Father God, thank You for this story as it reminds me of the importance of listening to Jesus. Amen.

Follow Me

Jesus' appearance changed when He was transfigured. Instead of changing our appearance, let's change our attitude for the day. Maybe you woke up feeling grouchy or complaining. If so, then transform your bad attitude into a good attitude. Practice having a good attitude this week in all that you do.

Listen to Him

Mark 9:7

"Then a cloud appeared and covered them, and a voice came from the cloud: 'This is my Son, whom I love. Listen to him!'" Mark 9:7

Do you ever wish that you could audibly hear the voice of God? Do you wish that you could have a conversation with Him where you could actually hear Him speaking to you?

I have to say that I wish I could! There are times in my life when I just wish God would speak loudly so I could hear Him. It would make things a lot easier, right?

We read yesterday the story of Jesus' Transfiguration—when His appearance changed and He was super bright. There with Him were three disciples (Peter, James, and John). Those disciples got to experience something pretty cool that day…they heard the voice of God!

"Then a cloud appeared and covered them, and a voice came from the cloud: 'This is my Son, whom I love. Listen to Him!'" (Mark 9:7).

What would your reaction have been if you were one of those disciples? Excited? Scared? Maybe a little freaked out? I think I might have experienced all those emotions. But I think I would have been most focused on what God said. It was pretty important and He wanted the disciples to hear it. And He wants us to hear this message, too…Listen to Jesus.

Even though we can't hear the voice of Jesus speak out loud, we can know when He talks to us. God gave us the Bible to read. That's how He directly communicates with us. But He also may send messages through prayer, through other people, through devotions you read, and He even speaks to us in the silence.

God sent us Jesus and He wants us to listen to Him. So take time today to be quiet and just listen for the voice of God. You won't be able to hear it out loud, but you'll hear His voice in your heart. You just have to be still and listen.

Father of All, thank You for sending Jesus to me. Help me to take time to be still and listen to You today. In Jesus' name, Amen.

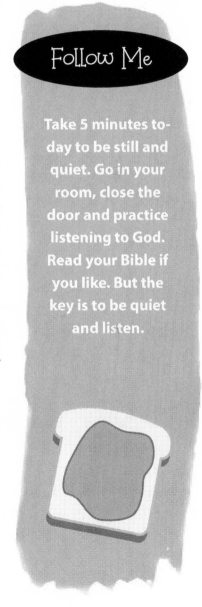

Follow Me

Take 5 minutes today to be still and quiet. Go in your room, close the door and practice listening to God. Read your Bible if you like. But the key is to be quiet and listen.

Jesus the Good Shepherd
John 10:1–6

"He calls his own sheep by name and leads them out."
John 10:3b

Do you like hearing your name called? Well…maybe not so much when you get in trouble by your parents or your teacher at school. But most of the time I think we really love to hear someone say our name. It makes us feel special…like we belong, like we are loved by others, like we are known.

Did you know that Jesus loves you and calls you by name?

In John chapter 10, we see a story that Jesus is sharing with the Pharisees. In this story He is talking about sheep and a shepherd. It might seem strange that Jesus is talking about this, but He is relating this story to our relationship with Him.

You see, Jesus is our shepherd, our Good Shepherd, and we are His sheep. In verse 3 it says that "He calls his own sheep by name and leads them out." He knows who you are. He knows your name. And He calls each one of us to follow Him.

Jesus goes on to say that sheep know the shepherd's voice. Hmmm…how do we know what Jesus' voice sounds like if we can't audibly hear it?

You may hear Jesus speaking to you through other ways like when you read the Bible, through your parents, teachers or friends, or sometimes you just get this overwhelming feeling that you should or should not do something. That's the Holy Spirit talking to you. When we believe in Jesus, we know His voice and we follow Him.

Remember that Jesus loves you and He knows your name. He calls you to follow Him. He wants to have a close relationship with you and He can do that if you are closely following Him. And that means doing things that you know are right and staying away from things you know are wrong.

Listen for Jesus' voice. He is calling your name.

Father God, I thank You for calling me to follow You. Help me to listen closely when You call my name. Teach me to obey all that You ask of me and to go wherever You lead me. In Jesus' name, Amen.

Follow Me

In a notebook, write your name in big letters. Then around your name, write down things you hear Jesus asking you to do. Finish by praying and asking Him to help you hear Him.

Parable of the Good Samaritan

Luke 10:25-37

"'Which of these three do you think was a neighbor to the man who fell into the hands of robbers?' The expert in the law replied, 'The one who had mercy on him.' Jesus told him, 'Go and do likewise.'" Luke 10:36-37

In the Parable of the Good Samaritan, we find Jesus talking with an expert in the law. Jesus shares with him the commandment to "Love your neighbor as yourself." (Luke 10:27b). Then the expert of the law asks Jesus, "And who is my neighbor?" (Luke 10:29b). That's when Jesus goes into the parable of the Good Samaritan.

A man was walking to Jericho and a bunch of robbers came upon him and beat him up. They hurt him badly enough that he was near death. Three different people came along that road and saw him: a priest, a Levite, and a Samaritan. You would think that the priest or Levite would be the one to help him because they were Jews just like this man, but they never stopped to help. The one who did help was a Samaritan who took him to an inn and took care of him and helped nurse him back to good health.

After Jesus tells them this story, He then says to go and be like the Samaritan who was a good neighbor to the man who was hurt. He was the one who loved him.

So who is your neighbor? Is it just the people who live next door to you or the ones who live in your neighborhood? Jesus would say it is any person in the whole world. Your neighbors are the ones who live next door to you, the ones who live in your city, the ones who live in your state, the ones who live in your country, and the ones who live on the other side of the world.

Jesus said for us to "go and do likewise" (Luke 10:37b), which means to take care of our neighbors just as the Samaritan did to the Jewish man. Talk with your parents about ways you can be a good neighbor. And go out today and be the hands and feet of Jesus.

Good Father, thank You for this story. Help me to be like the Samaritan and to be a good neighbor to those in need. Show me ways that I can help others. In Jesus' name, Amen.

Follow Me

Did you know there are children in other countries who cannot go to school or get medical help? You could help a child in need be able to do these things! Your family can sponsor a child and help pay for their education and medical needs. There are several great organizations your family can look into if they want to sponsor a child: Compassion International, World Vision, or the 410 Bridge.

Martha and Mary

Luke 10:38-42

"'Martha, Martha,' the Lord answered, 'you are worried and upset about many things, but few things are needed – or indeed only one. Mary has chosen what is better, and it will not be taken away from her.'" Luke 10:41-42

I love hosting parties! I love to have people at my house for dinner or to watch a game (we love football and soccer). I love to have my children's friends over to hang out and swim. I just love to have people at my house.

I think I might be a little bit like Martha in our story today. Martha and Mary are sisters who have opened their home for Jesus to come for a visit. Martha is busy preparing the food. She probably even took a lot of time cleaning the house before He arrived, too. (I do the same thing when I have people over!).

But she gets upset because her sister, Mary, is doing nothing to help her. She's not helping prepare the food at all. What is Mary doing then? She is sitting at the feet of Jesus listening to Him teach. Then Martha does something you may have done before to your sibling...she tattles on Mary! She goes up to Jesus and tells Him that Mary is not doing anything to help her around the house. And then she tells Jesus that He needs to make her help her. Would you have done the same thing?

Jesus uses this moment to teach Martha an important lesson. He tells her not to be worried or upset about all the things she feels she has to do. He tells her she needs to do only one thing...and that is to be like Mary and sit and listen to Him. Basically, He's telling her not to be so busy that she forgets the most important thing and that's listening and learning from Him.

Do you ever find that your life is busy and filled with lots of things? School, homework, projects, sports, dance, or music? Sometimes those things can fill your schedule where you feel like you don't even have 5 minutes to spend with Jesus. I pray you will work hard at making time each day to pray and read your Bible. Know that this is a very important part of being a good follower of Jesus. We must take time to learn and listen to Him.

Father God, thank You for the story of Martha and Mary. Help me to be more like Mary and take time to sit at Your feet and listen and learn from You. In Jesus' name, Amen.

Follow Me

Go to church on Sunday. You might be tired or want to sleep in but go to a worship service and then go to Sunday School or the children's program at your church. Take time to worship the Lord and spend time with Him.

Parable of the Great Banquet

Luke 14:15-24

"When one of those at the table with him heard this, he said to Jesus, 'Blessed is the one who will eat at the feast in the kingdom of God.'" Luke 14:15

Have you ever been to a nice banquet…one with a long table of food? A banquet is where you sit at a table with people you know, or even some you don't know, and get as many plates of food as you want, until your belly can hold no more.

This is the kind of banquet I believe is in our story today about the Parable of the Great Banquet. Jesus tells of a man who prepared a lot of food and invited many people to come. He sent his servants out to go and get the guests he invited and tell them that everything was ready.

But when the servants went out, all the guests the man had invited told them that they couldn't come. They gave excuse after excuse of why they couldn't come. Basically, they were too busy to be bothered about going to a great banquet.

So the man told his servants to go back out and invite anyone to his banquet. He told them to go out into the streets of the town and bring in "the poor, the crippled, the blind, and the lame." (Luke 14:21). He opened his banquet to anyone in the town. He just wanted people to come and eat.

Jesus relates this story to what it's like to eat at the feast in the kingdom of God. All people are invited to heaven to live with Jesus forever. But many people tell Jesus they are too busy or don't have time for Him, or even that they don't believe in Him. They throw away the invitation Jesus gives them and choose to do their own thing. It makes me sad to see people who choose not to believe in Jesus. I want everyone to come to know Jesus as their Savior.

I pray you will accept the invitation Jesus gives you to live forever with Him. Give Jesus your heart and follow Him. Spend time with Him daily and listen to Him. Then one day when you get to heaven you will eat at the great feast in the kingdom of God.

Jesus, thank You for inviting me to the great feast in heaven. Help me to accept this invitation and always follow You. In Your name I pray, Amen.

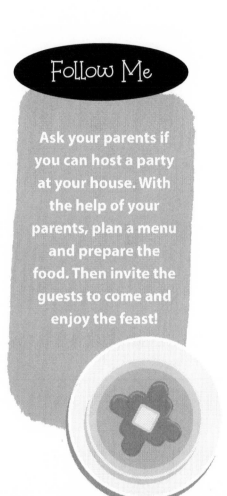

Follow Me

Ask your parents if you can host a party at your house. With the help of your parents, plan a menu and prepare the food. Then invite the guests to come and enjoy the feast!

Fruit Salad

You can use any fruit of your choice, but here are my favorite fruits to put in a fruit salad:

Bananas, diced	Strawberries, diced
Apples, diced	Kiwi, peeled and diced
Pineapple, diced	Peaches, diced
Grapes	Oranges, peeled and diced

Mix all fruit together in a large bowl and serve!

Something To Chew On

· · · · · · · · · · · · · · ·

**Who is your favorite Bible character
and why?**

Parable of the Lost Sheep
Luke 15:1-7

"I tell you that in the same way there will be more rejoicing in heaven over one sinner who repents than over ninety-nine righteous persons who do not need to repent."
Luke 15:7

Have you ever lost a toy before? Did you search for it or did you just consider it completely lost and give up?

If it's a toy you really loved, I am assuming you would keep searching until you found it. But even though you searched for it and couldn't find it, you considered it a lost cause and gave up. Was it really that important to you anyway?

I am so grateful that Jesus tells us that He will never stop looking for us if we are lost. We see this from the Parable of the Lost Sheep. A shepherd takes out his one hundred sheep. While he's out he loses one of them. So what does he do? He leaves behind the ninety-nine and goes in search for that one lost sheep. Why would he do that? Why does that one sheep matter so much?

When he finds the lost sheep, he rejoices and asks his friends to rejoice with him. The shepherd wants to have a celebration because his one sheep has been found. He loves all his sheep and is so thankful they are back with him.

In this story, Jesus is the Shepherd and we are the sheep. There may be times in your life when you get "lost," which means you stop following Jesus. You stop praying. You stop reading your Bible. You are lost and separated from Jesus.

I pray this will never happen to you. But if it ever does, know this…Jesus will never stop searching for you. He will work hard at bringing you back to Him. He will never give up or consider that you are a lost cause. Why? Because He loves you so very much. He wants you to follow Him always and to trust in Him.

What happens when Jesus finds that person who has gone away from Him? There is a lot of rejoicing and celebrating going on in heaven. The whole kingdom will rejoice that they have been found and are back in the arms of Jesus. Heaven will be a big party because a lost person has been found. What an awesome reason to celebrate!

Good Shepherd, thank You for never giving up on me even when I do things that are wrong. Forgive me and help me to always follow You. In Jesus' name, Amen.

Follow Me

Is there someone you know that has recently accepted Jesus into their heart or has been baptized? If you do know someone, why not throw a party for them? Invite them and some other friends to your home and celebrate them coming to know Jesus. It's a great reason to celebrate!

Parable of the Lost Coin
Luke 15:8-10

"In the same way, I tell you, there is rejoicing in the presence of the angels of God over one sinner who repents."
Luke 15:10

I found it! I found it! I am so thankful that I found my lost penny!

Let me be honest for a moment and say that I probably have never uttered those words in my life about a lost penny. Let's be real…pennies are not worth much. If I lose one, I really don't care. I definitely don't go tearing up my house in search for it. It's just not worth it to me.

The woman we see in today's parable is the opposite of me. I need to be more like her.

This woman has ten silver coins. Somehow one of those coins goes missing. This coin is precious to her and she wants to find it. So she sweeps the whole house and searches very carefully for it. I bet when she found that lost silver coin she might have even shouted the words I wrote above, "I found it! I found it! I am so thankful that I found my lost silver coin!" After she finds it, she goes and finds her neighbors and asks them to rejoice with her. It's an exciting day for her!

Jesus relates this story of finding a lost coin to the sinner (someone who does something wrong) who asks for forgiveness. Jesus says that there is much rejoicing in heaven when a sinner repents of their sins. It's definitely a day of rejoicing!

How often do you ask God for forgiveness of your sins? Maybe there are days you forget. And that's ok. Here's something that might help you remember to ask for forgiveness. Every day when I pray I start by praising God, then ask for forgiveness of my sins (even naming the sins out loud that I can remember), thank God for all the blessings He's given to me, pray for others, pray for myself, and then close by praising God again. This pattern of prayer time has helped me remember to repent of my sins daily.

We are sinners. We sin every day. But I am so grateful that we serve Jesus Christ who came to die for our sins and who forgives us every time when we do repent of the sins we have done. Remember to pray daily and ask Jesus to forgive you of all your sins. There will be a lot of rejoicing in heaven when you do.

Loving God, please forgive me of all the sins I have committed against You. Thank You for this story that helps me to see that You are happy when I come to You and seek forgiveness of my sins. Help me to remember to do this daily. In Jesus' name, Amen.

Follow Me

Find a piece of paper and write down sins that you remember committing. Pray and ask God to forgive you. Then take a red marker and write really big across them "FORGIVEN." This is a great visual reminder that Jesus has forgiven you.

Parable of the Lost Son
Luke 15:11-32

"But we had to celebrate and be glad, because this brother of yours was dead and is alive again; he was lost and is found." Luke 15:32

I feel confident in saying that if you have a brother or sister you fight with them. You get angry when they won't share toys. Or mad when they won't help you do something. Or perhaps you do something wrong and they tell your parents. You fight over what TV shows or movies to watch, who gets to play the video game, who gets to pick their seat in the car, and maybe even who gets to eat the last piece of pizza. There are so many things that your brother or sister do or that you do to your brother or sister that causes fighting.

In the Parable of the Lost Son that Jesus shares in today's lesson, we see two brothers who don't get along. The youngest brother decides he wants his share of his father's money now, so he asks his dad for it and then he moves out and goes out on his own. The older brother stays at home and works hard for his father in the field helping take care of the animals.

However, things don't work out so well for the younger brother and he spends all his money and has nothing left to live on. Then to make matters worse, a famine comes over the whole land (that's when there is not much food in the land). And the younger brother is in desperate need of food and is starving.

So he swallows his pride and returns home and begs his father to forgive him. But before he's able to do any of that his father runs and meets him on the road and is so glad to see him. When he asks his father to forgive him, he does something crazy...he tells his servants to prepare a feast because it's a day to celebrate!

When the older brother learns of this celebration, he is furious! Why would his father celebrate a son who did nothing right? If anyone deserved a celebration, it was him because he was the son who stayed with his father and worked hard for him.

This story is another way of Jesus explaining to us that He will always forgive us of our sins when we come to Him. In this story, Jesus is the forgiving father and we are the younger brother. It doesn't matter what we have done to sin against Him, He will always forgive us when we come to Him and ask Him for forgiveness. Why? Because He loves us so very much and wants nothing more than for us to be with Him forever in heaven. May you remember to seek forgiveness from Jesus today.

Lord Jesus, I ask that You forgive me of all my sins. Help me to stay close to You and follow You. I love You, Lord. Amen.

Follow Me

Practice showing forgiveness to your brother or sister today. If they do something to hurt you or annoy you, show them kindness and tell them you forgive them.
Then give them a great big hug!

Jesus Heals Ten Men

Luke 17:11-19

"One of them, when he saw he was healed, came back,
praising God in a loud voice. He threw himself at Jesus' feet and thanked him – and he was a Samaritan."
Luke 17:15-16

No one enjoys being sick. When you're sick you don't feel like playing outside; you want to lay on the couch, sleep, and watch movies. You also long to be well, for the medicine to work, or for the virus you have just to go away. You want to be healed.

The lepers that Jesus encountered in today's story longed to be well, too. Leprosy was a skin disease that created these scaly spots on your skin. It was very contagious so no one wanted to be around anyone who had leprosy. Lepers (people who had leprosy) had to live in their own towns. If they were wandering around others who did not have the disease, they had to shout "unclean" so that no one would get near them. They were considered outcasts and nobody wanted anything to do with them. But then Jesus came and He showed compassion to the lepers.

In this story, Jesus is traveling to Jerusalem along the border of Samaria and Galilee. As He was heading into a village, ten men with leprosy approached Him. Most people would have freaked out and yelled for them to get away, but not Jesus. I believe these lepers had heard stories that Jesus could heal and all they wanted was to be healed from this terrible disease.

Jesus shows compassion to them and tells them to go to the priests to be healed. And guess what? They were healed! Can you just imagine the reaction of these lepers after being healed? They had to be dancing and jumping and shouting for joy! I would think that all of them would have run back to find Jesus to thank Him for healing them.

But you know what? Only one of the ten men came back to thank Jesus. Only one! And this man who came back was a Samaritan (someone whom the Jews didn't like). Why didn't the other Jewish lepers come back to thank Jesus?

This story reminds me of our need to always give thanks to Jesus, especially after He heals us of our sickness. How many times have you thanked Jesus for healing you when you were sick? The thought might not have ever crossed your mind. But I hope this story will remind you to always thank Jesus, not only just when He has healed you, but even when you are well. We should continually thank Jesus for everything He gives us and everything He does for us.

Father God, thank You for the times You have brought healing to me when I am sick. Thank You for all You have given me. Help me to give thanks to You at all times. In Jesus' name, Amen.

Follow Me

Write a thank you note to Jesus. List all the things you are thankful for. Keep this note in your Bible and add to it each day.

Jesus and the Children
Mark 10:13-16

"And he took the children in his arms, placed his hands on them and blessed them." Mark 10:16

Imagine you are living back in Bible times. You are in a crowd of people with your parents. Your parents have heard about Jesus and they believe in Him. They believe that He is from God and has come to save everyone. They have brought you to this place with all these people today because they want you to receive a blessing from Jesus.

There are so many people standing around Jesus that you wonder if you'll ever get a chance to see Him up close. You and your parents really want to see Him! But then something happens that makes you think that might not ever happen. His disciples start telling people to back away. They say that Jesus doesn't have time to bless children. There are too many people there and He must attend to other matters. They start telling you and your parents to leave.

When Jesus sees what the disciples are doing, He becomes angry! He can't believe that His friends are telling people to go away from Him, especially children. He loves children and He wants them to know that He cares for them, too.

Then He says something that brings a smile back to your face. "Let the little children come to me, and do not hinder them, for the kingdom of God belongs to such as these." (Mark 10:14). Then Jesus sees you and the other children and motions you to come to Him. He surrounds all of you with His arms and gives you a big hug. Then

He places His hand on each one of you and says a special blessing. What a powerful moment for you and the other kids.

I want you to remember this story found in the book of Mark. When there are times you feel like you don't matter to Jesus…read this story. When there are times you feel like nobody loves you… read this story. When there are times when you feel like you are not important…read this story. When there are times when all you want is for Jesus to hear you and see you…read this story. This story will remind you of all those things. You matter to Jesus. You are loved by Jesus. You are important to Jesus. Jesus sees and hears you.

I'll close with a song from my childhood that reminds me of Jesus' love for all children:

"Jesus loves the little children, all the children of the world. Red and yellow, black and white, they are precious in His sight. Jesus loves the little children of the world."

Thank You, Jesus, for loving me. Help me to remember that at all times. Amen.

Follow Me

Make a video of yourself sharing with others why Jesus loves them. Then send that video to a friend or family member who needs to be reminded that Jesus loves them.

The Rich Man and the Kingdom of God

Matthew 19:16–26

"Jesus looked at them and said, 'With man this is impossible, but with God all things are possible.'" Matthew 19:26

Some things just seem impossible, right? Making a basketball goal from half court, kicking a 60-yard field goal, cleaning your room, getting that muddy stain out of your white shirt, eating all the spinach on your dinner plate, figuring out that confusing math problem on your homework. There are so many things you think can't be done.

That's how the rich man felt when he asked Jesus the question, "Teacher, what good thing must I do to get eternal life?" (Matthew 19:16). Jesus' answer was to keep all the commandments. The man said he did all that. But then Jesus said one thing that he didn't really want to do. Jesus asked him to go sell all his possessions and give to the poor.

You see, this man was very wealthy. He had a lot of money and was not sure if he could give up all his money plus all his possessions to follow Jesus. It seemed impossible.

Jesus then goes on to say that "it is easier for a camel to go through the eye of a needle than for someone who is rich to enter the kingdom of God." (Matthew 19:24). When the disciples heard Jesus say that, they asked Him who then could be saved, because what He just said seemed impossible!

Jesus explains that "with man this is impossible, but with God all things are possible." (Matthew 19:26). Our minds can't imagine even doing what Jesus said. How could we give up everything to follow Him? I don't think Jesus was saying that this man really needed to give away every single thing he owned. But Jesus was saying that he needed to give up his wealth and share with others.

What are some things you love and can't imagine having to give up? Maybe those are the things that God is calling you to give up so you can have a closer relationship with Him. Maybe those are the things that are keeping you from walking with Jesus. I encourage you to think about what those things may be and then pray and ask God to help you give it up. That might be a video game you play all the time, a TV show you watch that isn't something you really should be watching or saying ugly words to your brother or sister. No matter what it is, listen to God and follow Him. He can help you get through what seems impossible.

God of All, what things are keeping me from drawing closer to You? Show me what those things are and help me to see that it is possible to give up so I can follow You with all my heart. Amen.

Follow Me

Do you eat out at restaurants? Or get ice cream a lot? Think about giving up one time a week that you eat out or eat ice cream. Take the money you would normally use for it and give it to your church or an organization that feeds the homeless people.

Homemade Biscuits

2 cups self-rising flour
½ cup buttermilk
2 Tbsp. vegetable oil

Mix ingredients and add enough water to moisten and smooth mixture. Use a large tablespoon to spoon mixture in a pan sprayed with Pam. Bake at 400° in pre-heated oven till golden brown. Makes 8 biscuits. These are great served with apple butter.

Something To Chew On

· · · · · · · · · · · · · · · · · ·

How can you rise up and serve the
Lord today?

Parable of the Workers in the Vineyard
Matthew 20:1-16

"So the last will be first, and the first will be last."
Matthew 20:16

Imagine this scenario: You have been hired to do a job. You were hired at 9:00 am. When your boss sees there is a lot more work to do, he goes out and finds some help for you. The others start working at 12:00 pm. But then he sees that you need even more help, so he hires more workers and they start working at 3:00 pm. Then he goes out one more time to find you help (it's a big job), and those workers start at 6:00 pm.

The day comes to an end and it's time for everyone to be paid. The boss pays the 6:00 workers first and they get $100. Then he pays the 3:00 workers and they get $100. Then he pays the 12:00 workers and they get $100. By the time the 9:00 workers get paid, you are thinking that your paycheck will be more than $100 because you worked the longest. But guess what…you only get paid $100, too! You are very upset! You don't understand why everyone got paid the same amount. You worked way longer than anyone else and you deserve more money. It's just not fair!

I'm sure you have heard your parents or your teacher say that "life's not fair." Don't you hate it when they say that? Why isn't life fair? Why won't you be paid the most if you work the longest? It just isn't right!

I believe Jesus told this parable to say one thing to us…everyone who believes in Jesus and accepts Him as their Savior will live in heaven forever with Him. It doesn't matter if they start believing in Him when they are 5 or when they are 75. No matter how long they have believed in Jesus, all of God's children will live in heaven if they believe in Him. And we should not be upset if we have accepted Jesus as a child and another person doesn't believe until they are really old.

Jesus wants all His children to believe in Him and is so happy when they do, no matter what age they are. He loves us all the same. Let's remember that and do our best to let others know about Him so they can believe in Him and live in heaven one day, too.

Almighty God, thank You for accepting all of us that believe in You. Help me to be a good witness and let others know that You are our Savior. In Jesus' name, Amen.

Follow Me

Do you get an allowance for doing chores? If you do, save up your allowance and then give it to someone in need. This could be someone who needs help buying groceries, someone who needs help with gas money for their car, or someone who can't afford to buy new clothes. No matter what it is, give your money to help another child of God.

Lazarus' Death

John 11:1-16

"When he heard this, Jesus said, 'This sickness will not end in death. No, it is for God's glory so that God's Son may be glorified through it.'" John 11:4

What do you do when you learn someone is sick? And I mean really sick…like when someone is in the hospital?

If you know them really well, you and your parents might go visit them in the hospital. Perhaps you send them a get—well card or some balloons. You probably also pray for them…maybe around the dinner table with your family or at bedtime. Your parents may even make a nice dinner and take it to their family so they don't have to worry about cooking dinner (something that is helpful to family members who have loved ones who are sick).

Lazarus was the brother of Mary and Martha. He was a good friend of Jesus. Jesus loved Lazarus and his sisters. They were close friends. When Jesus got word that His friend Lazarus was sick, He probably was sad. The Bible doesn't tell us. But what it does say is what we find in verse 4 above. Jesus tells us that Lazarus' sickness will not end in death, but it will all be for God's glory. His disciples probably had no clue what Jesus was really talking about.

What do you think Jesus did after He found out Lazarus was sick? Do you think He left where He was and went straight to Lazarus' house?

No, He didn't! He stayed where He was for two whole days! Can you believe it? Why would Jesus sit around for two days and not do anything to help His sick friend? It just doesn't make any sense, does it?

But what I love about Jesus is that He has a reason for everything He does. We don't always understand why He does what He does (or doesn't do in this case). We don't (and never will) understand or know why Jesus does things. There was a reason why Jesus waited two days to go to find Lazarus and visit with him. And we will see that reason be made known to us in tomorrow's devotion.

So if you are confused and don't know why something is happening in your life, just trust Jesus. Know that He's got it under control and will work all things for good.

Gracious and Loving God, I confess that sometimes I don't understand why certain things happen. Help me not to worry but to trust in You. In Jesus' name, Amen.

Follow Me

Know someone who is sick? With the help of your parents, cook them a meal and take it to them. You will be helping bless someone!

Jesus Wept
John 11:17-27

"Jesus wept." John 11:35

I can't help it.

Whenever I see someone who is crying, I usually shed a few tears myself. I feel so sad for them that the tears just seem to easily flow down my face.

Have you ever felt that way before when you see a friend who is sad? Do you ever cry with them?

Did you ever think that Jesus, the Savior of the world, would get sad? It's not something you usually picture when thinking about Jesus. But Jesus did cry. He felt compassion and sadness for those who were hurting.

In today's story, we pick back up with Lazarus. Remember, Jesus has just learned that Lazarus is sick, but instead of going straight to him to heal him, he waits around an extra two days. So when he arrives in Bethany (the village where Lazarus lived with his sisters, Martha and Mary), He finds out that Lazarus has been dead for four days! Martha and Mary are a little upset because Jesus didn't come right away to heal their brother. They believe that Lazarus would have never died if Jesus had gotten there earlier.

Mary shows her emotion and begins sobbing in front of Jesus. She is extremely upset that Lazarus has died. And then Jesus does something we don't usually see. "Jesus wept." (John 11:35 is the shortest verse in the Bible). Jesus has so much compassion for Mary that He begins crying, just as Mary is crying. I like to picture Jesus giving Mary a big hug and they both have a good cry together. The people in the crowd noticed His tears, too, and began to talk about how much Jesus loved Lazarus (He and Lazarus were good buddies).

This story shows all of us how much Jesus loves us and how much He felt emotion, just like everyone else. He cares for us and He cries with us when we are sad. Next time you are upset and crying, just remember how much Jesus loves you and cares for you. Aren't you thankful that we serve a God who cares so much for us?

Loving God, thank You for caring so much for me. Help me to re-member that You are with me at all times. In Jesus' name, Amen.

Follow Me

Hug a friend or a family member today if you see them upset or crying. Remind them how much Jesus loves them.

Another Miracle

John 11:38-44

"When he had said this, Jesus called in a loud voice, 'Lazarus, come out!' The dead man came out, his hands and feet wrapped with strips of linen, and a cloth around his face. Jesus said to them, 'Take off the grave clothes and let him go.'" John 11:43-44

One thing that every one of His disciples knows by this point in Jesus' life is that He can perform miracles. They have either watched Him do it or they have heard about Him doing it. They have watched Him change water into wine, heal the sick, let the blind see and the deaf hear, allowed the paralyzed to walk again, and cured people of leprosy. And now they were getting ready to witness a man rise from the dead.

Remember Lazarus…he's been dead for four days and his body has been put in a tomb. Jesus finally gets to his house and everyone is so upset because they feel that had Jesus been there days earlier, Lazarus would not have died. And remember that Jesus is sad, too. He loved Lazarus like a brother.

Jesus then went to the grave and told them to roll away the stone. Martha was a little surprised He said this because he had been dead for four days and it would really stink in the tomb! But Jesus still told them to roll away the stone and then He cried out, "Lazarus, come out!" (John 11:43).

And guess what…Lazarus came walking out of the grave! It was a miracle! Jesus had raised a person from the dead! I can only imagine the astonished looks on the faces of the friends who gathered to mourn the loss of Lazarus. No longer was their friend dead, he was alive!

You might be wondering why Lazarus actually died. What was God's plan in all this? Lazarus didn't die because Jesus didn't care enough to get there to help him. Nor did he die because Jesus couldn't heal him. Lazarus died so that God's glory would be revealed and so that others would come to believe in Jesus because of what He was about to do. If you read verse 45 in this chapter it even tells us that "many of the Jews who had come to visit Mary, and had seen what Jesus did, believed in him." Isn't that cool! Other people came to know Jesus and believe in Him because they saw Lazarus being raised from the dead. They knew that Jesus was the Son of God.

Maybe there are things that happen in your life that don't exactly go as planned. You were hoping that one thing would happen and were sad when it didn't turn out like you wanted. But then something even better happened and now you know that God had a plan for it all. Remember that God's plan is always BETTER than anything we can ever hope or imagine. We just have to trust in God and believe in Him.

Loving God, help me to remember to always believe in You even when things don't turn out the way I plan. Thank You for loving me so very much. In Jesus' name, Amen.

Follow Me

Plan a fun outing with your family. Go to your favorite restaurant, a water park, the movies, or even help plan your next vacation. Remember that when things don't go exactly as planned, God's plans are always better than anything we could ever plan ourselves.

Jesus Predicts His Death
Matthew 20:17-19

"Now Jesus was going up to Jerusalem. On the way, he took
the Twelve aside and said to them, 'We are going up to Jerusalem, and the Son of Man will be delivered over to the chief
priests and the teachers of the law. They will condemn him to
death and will hand him over to the Gentiles to be mocked
and flogged and crucified. On the third day he will be raised
to life!" Matthew 20:17-19

There is nobody in the whole entire world that can predict the
day they will leave this earth and be joined with Jesus in heaven.

Well…no one except Jesus, that is.

Jesus was born on this earth for one reason…to save us from
our sins. And He knew everything that would happen to Him while
on this earth. He knew who would be the ones to crucify Him and
the ones who would believe in Him. He knew the number of days
He would live. He knew how He would die. He knew how much He
would suffer before He died. Jesus knew everything that would
happen to Him while He was alive on this earth.

Jesus knew all this and He made sure to tell His twelve disciples
all this, too. I believe He wanted to prepare them for what was to
come. It's like He wanted to give them a heads up to let them know
what was going to happen so they wouldn't be surprised.

Jesus let the disciples know this three different times that we
read about in the Bible (Matthew 16:21, Matthew 17:22-23, Matthew 20:17-19). He knew that one time wouldn't be enough. He

knew they wouldn't believe Him if He said it once so He made sure to repeat it again and again to them.

But you know what? They still didn't believe any of what Jesus said was going to happen to Him. Maybe they thought it sounded so outrageous that it would surely never happen to Jesus, the Son of God…the One who could perform any miracle…the One who loved everyone. Surely their Jesus would never die in the way He said.

But we know it did. And we know how the story ends. Jesus is alive! Praise be to God for sending His Son to save us from our sins.

Heavenly Father, thank You for sending Jesus to die for me. Help me to remember that Your Word is true and to always believe it. Amen.

Follow Me

Visit a nursing home or assisted living home with your family or church group. Spend time visiting with the residents and letting them know that Jesus loves them.

A Mother's Request
Matthew 20:20-28

"Instead, whoever wants to become great among you must be your servant." Matthew 20:26

Do you know that your parents would do anything for you? They love you so much and want to provide you with only the best.

I believe that is what the mother of James and John wanted, too. She wanted only the best for her two sons. James and John were two of Jesus' disciples. They were called to follow Jesus and learn from Him. They left behind their lives of being fishermen to follow the One who could bring eternal life.

I know that the mother of James and John loved them so very much and that is why she asked Jesus for a favor. Now…let me just say that what she asks is very bold and something I'm not sure I would have asked for my own kids.

In verse 21 she asks, "Grant that one of these two sons of mine may sit at your right and the other at your left in your kingdom." Wow! Can you believe she asked that? When the disciples found out what she asked they were less than pleased. Why would James & John's mother ask something like that?

But in her asking, Jesus explains a very important lesson for all of us. He tells her that what she asked is not His decision to make…it's God's. And then He goes on to explain that we all must be servants, just like He came to be a servant on this earth.

Sometimes we don't act like good servants, do we? Sometimes we think we are better than others because of the way we dress, the house we live in, the church we go to, the car our parents drive, or by the amount of money we might have stored up in our piggy banks. Jesus is saying here that we don't need to act like we are better than others because of these things. He calls us to live a life as a servant to others. Putting others first and serving them is what God wants.

Lord of All, forgive me when I think of myself more than I think of others. Help me to be more loving and to serve You by serving all people. In Jesus' name, Amen.

Follow Me

Practice putting others first before yourself today. Hold the door open for your classmates. Let a friend be the line leader. Help a friend with their home-work if they don't understand it. These types of acts will help you put others first.

Strawberry Banana Smoothie

9-10 strawberries (frozen work best)
1 banana, sliced
1 cup vanilla yogurt
Milk

In a blender, chop the frozen strawberries. Add bananas and yogurt. Blend till smooth. Add milk if desired for a creamier taste. Add a few pieces of ice if not using frozen strawberries. Serve immediately.

Something To Chew On

What parts of your life seem frozen and cut off from God?

Blind Bartimaeus
Mark 10:46–52

"'What do you want me to do for you?' Jesus asked him. The blind man said, 'Rabbi, I want to see.'" Mark 10:51

A blind man named Bartimaeus sat by the roadside day after day begging for help. He needed food, but what he really wanted most was to be able to see. If he could just see, then his life would be so much better.

One day as he sat on the road he heard people saying the name of Jesus. He had heard about this Jesus because others had talked about the healings and miracles that He could perform. They kept saying that Jesus was walking down the road…the same road where he was sitting. He immediately became excited and knew he had to see Jesus. So he began shouting, "Jesus, Son of David, have mercy on me!" (Mark 10:47). But for some reason the crowd of people around him kept telling him to be quiet. Why would he be quiet when Jesus was near? This made him shout even louder! He wanted to see Jesus!

And then the best thing happened…Jesus called Bartimaeus to come to Him. He leaped up and found his way to Jesus. When he got to Jesus, Jesus asked him one question, "What do you want me to do for you?" (Luke 10:51). The blind man knew the answer to that one immediately. It's something he had been wanting for a long time. "Rabbi, I want to see." (Luke 10:51). And you know what happened immediately? The blind man could see! The one thing he had been wanting for a very long time was to regain his sight. Praise be to Jesus who brought healing to him!

The blind man's answer to Jesus' question has become a prayer of mine. I pray for the Lord to help me see. I am not blind. I can see perfectly fine, but my prayer is for Jesus to help me see Him in everything. I want to see Him in creation. I want to see Him in others. I want others to see Him in me. I want Jesus to help me see Him everywhere I go.

If you've ever been to VBS, you might have heard people talk about God Sightings.[2] These are ways you have seen God in your day. Share these with your family each night or write them down in your journal. Every morning as you say your prayers, ask God to help you see Him that day. Keep your eyes and your heart open for Him to show Himself to you. You will be amazed at how many times you see God!

Creator God, help me to open my eyes and heart to see You today. Show me who You are and allow me to experience You in amazing ways. Amen.

---

2 Group Publishing Easy VBS, www.groupvbs.com

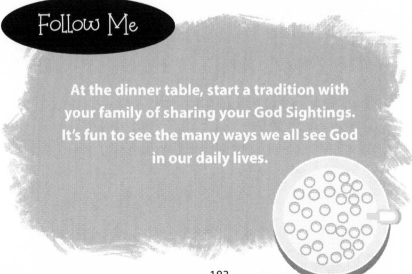

Follow Me

At the dinner table, start a tradition with your family of sharing your God Sightings. It's fun to see the many ways we all see God in our daily lives.

Zacchaeus

Luke 19:1–10

"When Jesus reached the spot, he looked up and said to him, 'Zacchaeus, come down immediately. I must stay at your house today.'" Luke 19:5

"I can't see, Daddy!"

Those were the words my oldest daughter screamed as we watched one of the parades at Disney World. I wondered why she was screaming that because I felt she had a great spot to view the parade that we were watching. But what she really wanted was to see far off. She wanted to catch a glimpse of all the parade floats and characters so she could yell back at us who was coming up. She wanted to have the best view possible.

And that's exactly what our friend, Zacchaeus, wanted. He had heard Jesus was coming into town. But there were so many people who were crowding the streets that he couldn't see a thing. It didn't help that he was shorter than others so seeing Jesus was going to be very difficult. So he did the one thing he knew to do in order to see Jesus…he climbed a sycamore tree. From atop that tree he could definitely see Jesus.

As Jesus began walking his way, He stopped and looked up and began talking to Zacchaeus. Jesus told him to come down because He wanted to eat at his house today. I am sure Zacchaeus was thrilled! He just wanted to be able to see Jesus. He wasn't expecting Jesus to talk to him, much less eat at his house! Because of Jesus' visit, Zacchaeus repented of his sins (he was a tax collector and stole money from people) and he came to believe in Jesus.

What I want you to remember from this story is that it doesn't matter what kind of sins you have committed; Jesus still loves you and wants you to believe in Him. Zacchaeus had done some terrible things by stealing money from people. Basically, he charged people extra in taxes and kept the extra part for himself! Not cool, Zacchaeus! But that didn't matter to Jesus. He forgave him and Zacchaeus believed in Jesus as his Savior. And because of what Jesus did for him, Zacchaeus said that he would re-pay everyone back that he stole from and he would give them back four times as much money as he took from them. How amazing!

Glorious God, thank You for forgiving Zacchaeus of his sins. Please forgive me of what I have done wrong, too. Help me to live my life for You. In Jesus' name, Amen.

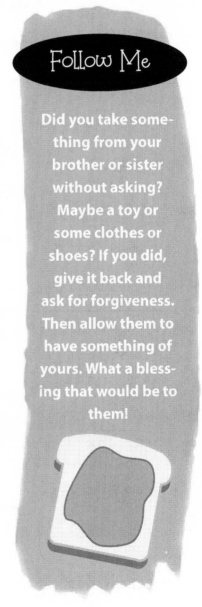

Follow Me

Did you take something from your brother or sister without asking? Maybe a toy or some clothes or shoes? If you did, give it back and ask for forgiveness. Then allow them to have something of yours. What a blessing that would be to them!

75

The Triumphal Entry

Matthew 21:1–11

"The crowds that went ahead of him and those that followed shouted, 'Hosanna to the Son of David! Blessed is he who comes in the name of the Lord! Hosanna in the highest heaven!'" Matthew 21:9

If you've ever seen a famous person before, what did you do? You probably had your camera ready and began snapping tons of pictures (or maybe even selfies) with this celebrity. I am pretty sure you screamed and yelled and cheered loudly for them. You may have even stuck out your hand to see if they would give you a high five as they passed by. You were probably super excited to see this famous person.

Jesus was pretty famous in His day. Many people knew who He was and what He could do. Anytime He came into their town, they found Him and followed Him around. I am sure the crowd of people still cheered and shouted His name, but there were no selfies with Jesus since there was no such thing as a camera!

Jesus was entering the city of Jerusalem. People lined the road into town and did something we probably would never do…they laid down their cloaks (coats) and picked up palm branches and began shouting. They were shouting "Hosanna to the Son of David! Blessed is he who comes in the name of the Lord! Hosanna in the highest heaven." (Matthew 21:9).

Seems a little odd, right? But it really wasn't! Jesus was the King of the Jews so they praised Him. Their act of laying down their cloaks symbolized honor for a king. And the palm branches were waved because they symbolized victory and were used to honor royalty. Since Jesus was King of the Jews, He was royalty and deserved all their honor and praise. This act of laying down cloaks and waving palm branches was their way of giving honor to Jesus and praising Him.

What do you do today to honor Jesus and to give praise to Him? Think about some things that you could do to give praise to Jesus. Write those down and remember to do them. Jesus deserves all our praise, glory, and honor.

Almighty God, I praise You today. I give honor and glory to Your name. Help me to always praise You. Amen.

Follow Me

Create a Praise Jar for your family. At dinner time each night, give each family member a small piece of paper to write down something they want to praise Jesus for that day. Then fold them up and put into your family's Praise Jar. When the jar gets full, go back through together as a family and praise God.

76

The Widow's Offering

Luke 21:1-4

"All these people gave their gifts out of their wealth;
but she out of her poverty put in all she had to live on."
Luke 21:4

When I was a kid, my parents divorced. At that time my mother was not working, so in order for her to start teaching again (she had once been a teacher before she had kids), she had to go back to school and take a few more classes. For two years my mother worked at a preschool and took classes at night. Let's just say that we didn't have much money. I couldn't get everything I wanted and I couldn't do everything I wanted to do. Money was tight.

But one thing I remember is that my mom continued to give an offering to the church. She taught us that you always give to God... even when you feel like you won't have enough money to pay all your bills. We give to God because it's a way of giving honor to Him. And when we honor and give to Him, God gives back to us and blesses us. I may not have gotten everything I wanted, but I know that God provided everything I needed. I had food to eat, clean water to drink, a place to sleep, and clothes to wear. I had all that because God provided it for my family.

There was a widow (someone whose husband has died) who didn't have very much money at all. She came to the temple to give her money to God as an offering. At the same time, there were many others who came to the temple to give an offering as well. But these people were wealthy. They gave money because they had money to give. They weren't poor like the widow. They didn't worry about what they would eat if they gave their money to the temple. This widow put in the only two copper coins she had. They weren't worth very much, but she gave because she wanted to honor God with her gifts.

Jesus saw all this from where He was standing in the temple, and He told His disciples that the widow gave more than the wealthy did because she gave all she had. We know that she fully trusted in God because she gave Him everything she had. And because of this, she knew that God would provide for her. The Bible doesn't go on to say how God provided for her, but I know without a doubt, that God gave her all she needed…just like He did for me and my family.

When you honor God with your gifts, He will bless you and provide for you. I believe this because I have seen His many blessings given to me…when I was a child and even today. God is so good!

Giving God, help me to always honor You with my offerings. Help me to give to You at all times, just like the widow. Amen.

Follow Me

One of the things I loved to do as a child was put money into the offering plate at church. The next time you go to church, ask your parents for some money (or take some of your own allowance), and place it in the offering plate. This is a way of giving to God.

Jesus at the Temple
Matthew 21:12-17

"'It is written,' he said to them, 'My house will be called a house of prayer, but you are making it a 'den of robbers.'"
Matthew 21:13

Think about a time when your parents have gotten mad at you. You might have broken something, lied to them, not cleaned your room, or done something you know you shouldn't have done. This caused them to be angry with you. I am sure there was some yelling involved and you probably got grounded from something, like watching TV or playing video games. It's no fun when you get in trouble, is it?

When you think about Jesus, I bet you never think about Him getting angry, do you? But you know what...there was a time in the Bible where He got extremely upset.

Jesus went to the temple in Jerusalem one day. He went there to pray, but what He found upset Him greatly. He saw people who had set up tables inside the temple court. These people were selling doves and animals that were needed for the Passover sacrifice.

There were also men called money changers who were exchanging money in the temple. To buy the required sacrifices to make in the temple, you had to pay with Hebrew coins. If you didn't have Hebrew coins you had to visit the money changer table and exchange what you had for a Hebrew coin. What was bad about this was that they charged an extra fee (something that was against the law).[3]

3 https://www.patheos.com/blogs/davearmstrong/2019/09/why-did-jesus-cleanse-the-temple-moneychangers.html

Does the temple seem like a good place to do these things? Of course not! And Jesus wasn't about to let anything like that go on in the temple.

Jesus is upset and begins yelling. He tells people to get out. And then He overturns tables and things start flying everywhere. It had to be an awkward scene for sure. I mean…animals were going all over the place!

But Jesus did this to remind people that the temple was not meant for selling things. It's not a place to make money or take advantage of people by charging more for things than normal. It's a place where people can go to confess their sins and talk to God. Jesus wanted to make sure people were using the temple as it should be used…a house of prayer and not as a den of robbers.

Loving God, thank You for reminding me what church is. Help me to use Your church as a house of prayer at all times. In Jesus' name, Amen.

Follow Me

As a family, have each person write down a prayer request at the beginning of the week. Then put them in a hat and have everyone draw one out. That's what you will pray for all week. At the end of the week, come back and talk about how God is answering that prayer.

Give to God
Mark 12:17

"Then Jesus said to them, 'Give back to Caesar what is Caesar's and to God what is God's.' And they were amazed at him." Mark 12:17

You've got a piggy bank full of money that you have been saving for something special. You've been wanting this one thing for a long time but then your mom mentions something to you about how you need to give some of that money to God. Why do you have to give money to God? Does He really need your money?

The answer to that is yes.

In Mark 12, we see a group of Pharisees (religious teachers) asking Jesus about whether they must pay taxes to the government. Jesus goes on to say that yes, you do need to pay taxes to the government. But, you also need to give to God what is God's.

So what is God's?

God asks us to give a tithe of our money to Him. You can find that in Leviticus 27:30. A tithe is 10% of whatever money we have. So if you have $100 saved up, you would give God $10.

God doesn't ask for much, but sometimes we have a hard time letting go of that 10%. We want to cling to it and buy what we want without giving God any of it. My challenge to you is to practice saving the money you get from chores or allowances. And then every week or every month (however often you want to give your offering to God), take 10% of your savings and give it to Him. That could be as an offering at your church, to help a charity organization, to give food to the poor, or even to a family or friend who needs financial help.

Will you accept the challenge?

Faithful God, thank You for all that You have given to me. Help me to remember to give a tithe to You. Remind me to be faithful to You in my giving as You are always faithful in giving to me. In Jesus' name, Amen.

Follow Me

Get 2 jars for saving your money. On one jar write "Savings". On the other jar write "Give to God." As you get money, put a tenth into God's jar and the rest in your savings jar. Then at the end of the month, give all the money in your Give to God jar to God.

Breakfast Burrito

Your choice of meat (bacon, ham, sausage, chicken)
2 eggs, scrambled
Soft tortillas
Grated cheese
Salsa

Cook thoroughly the meat you plan to use. Scramble 2 eggs. On a soft tortilla, layer meat, scrambled eggs, grated cheese and salsa. Wrap the tortilla and eat!

Something To Chew On

· · · · · · · · · · · · · · · · · ·

**What type of breakfast burrito would
you serve to Jesus?**

On Whose Authority?
Matthew 21:23-27

"Jesus entered the temple courts, and, while he was teaching, the chief priests and the elders of the people came to him. 'By what authority are you doing these things?' they asked. 'And who gave you this authority?'" Matthew 21:23

"Who said you could have your phone back?"

That's the question I asked my daughter when I came home to find her with her phone that I knew I had grounded her from. I wanted to know who gave her permission to have it back because I knew it wasn't me!

There may be times in your life when you have been asked that same question…Who gave you permission to do that? Basically, they're asking you who gave you the authority to do that. And that's the question Jesus was asked by the chief priests when He began His teaching in the temple.

We find Jesus having entered Jerusalem on a donkey, going to the temple to clear it of the people selling things, and then He begins His teaching in the temple. The chief priests and elders of the people were surprised, shocked, and amazed that He was doing these things and they wanted to know one thing, "And who gave you this authority?" (Matthew 21:23b). They didn't think He should be doing or saying some of the things He was teaching about. Who did this guy think He was?

What I love about Jesus is that He doesn't give them a straight answer when they ask. He comes back with a question. He says that if they answer His question correctly then He'll tell them by what authority He is teaching. And the question He asks have the chief priests and elders all confused and afraid of giving the wrong answer. So they just come back with an "I don't know." And guess what? Jesus said He wasn't going to tell them who gives Him authority either.

I'm sure the chief priests and elders slumped away, upset and angry at Jesus. They don't like His teaching and they don't like how He never answers their questions. Even if Jesus did come back with the answer to their question, do you think they would have believed Him?

Jesus receives His authority from God. But for some reason, these priests couldn't grasp that Jesus was the Son of God and that He came into the world to save all people. They felt like He wasn't telling the truth. But we know that Jesus was telling the truth and that Jesus is the Truth. Never doubt Jesus and His love for you.

God of Truth, help me to never doubt You. Help me to always believe in You even when others around me do not. Thank You for all You teach me in Your Word. Amen.

Follow Me

Write thank you notes to your local police officers. Bake a fresh batch of cookies and deliver them with your thank you notes.

He is Coming Again
Matthew 24:36,42,44

"Therefore keep watch, because you do not know on what day your Lord will come." Matthew 24:42

Ready or not, here I come!

Those words always brought butterflies to my stomach when I would play hide and seek with my friends when I was a kid. The seeker would count and no matter if I was hidden or not, they were coming to find me! Sometimes I was ready and well hidden. And other times I was not. The anticipation of the seeker finding me made me so nervous! If I saw the seeker and they saw me, then I would scream and try to run to base, hoping I would make it there before getting caught. Sometimes I made it. Sometimes I did not.

The one thing that is important for anyone playing hide and seek is for the player to be ready. If you are not hidden, then chances are you won't be winning the game. You must be ready.

This is what we must remember when we hear about God's promise to come again. Jesus says in these verses in Matthew 24 that we must be ready. There is no piddling around (a phrase my mother always used when I wasn't getting ready for school). We don't need to be standing around trying to figure out what to do. We can't decide to accept Jesus as our Savior and then not follow His ways. We must be all in and be ready.

We also have no idea when the coming of the Lord will happen. Jesus tells us it will be at an hour we don't expect. There is no way we can predict when this will happen. Jesus says that the angels don't know and even He, Jesus, doesn't know. Only the Father knows when He will come again.

I want to be ready for that day. And I want you to be ready, too. We can do this by following Jesus every day of our lives, doing what we know is right and what we know Jesus would want us to do, spending time with Him every day, praying, praising Him, worshiping Him at church, and learning more about Him as we read the Bible. Let's all be ready because we know that one day Jesus will come again!

Almighty God, thank You for the promise You give that You will come again. Help me to live my life every day for You. In Jesus' name, Amen.

Follow Me

Jesus calls us to worship and praise Him. Let's make today be praise and worship day! Every time you get in your car with your family, turn on praise music on your radio, mp3 player, phone, CD player, or other device. Let's sing loudly in praise and honor for Jesus!

The Anointing of Jesus

Matthew 26:6-13

"Truly I tell you, wherever this gospel is preached throughout the world, what she has done will also be told, in memory of her." Matthew 26:13

Let's picture this: your mother has just bought some new perfume. It smells so good that you decide you want to use some of it while you play. You spray some on yourself but then you come up with the idea of using it on your dolls. They need to smell good, too. But instead of spraying them with the perfume, you decide to pour the perfume over them.

When your mother comes in to find half the bottle of perfume gone, she is quite upset! She yells at you and says that cost her a lot of money and she can't believe you used so much of it! Not a good day for you.

The way your mother felt is the exact way the disciples felt the day they were at Simon the Leper's house. Jesus was with them and this woman came in with a jar of very expensive perfume. They were so upset when she opened the bottle and started pouring it over Jesus' head. They knew how much that perfume cost and couldn't believe she was wasting it like that! It could have been sold and the money given to the poor.

The disciples had no idea what she was doing, but Jesus did. You see, this woman was preparing Jesus' body for burial. She was anointing Him because He knew He would die soon. They didn't understand that and got upset with her.

But Jesus stood up for her and said what she was doing was appropriate. This act would be the thing that she would be known for. And guess what -- we do know this woman for what she did for Jesus as she poured perfume over His head to prepare Him for burial. It was an act of love she did to show Jesus she loved Him.

Gracious God, help me to always show my love for You. In Jesus' name, Amen.

Follow Me

Show an act of love to Jesus today. It could be something like being kind to others, spending time with Him, or simply bowing your head and telling Jesus you love Him.

Judas Agrees to Betray Jesus

Luke 22:1-6

"And Judas went to the chief priests and the officers of the temple guard and discussed with them how he might betray Jesus." Luke 22:4

What happens when someone you love or know does something wrong? You probably get sad, but I bet the first emotion you feel is anger. You are so mad at them for what they did or how they treated you or someone you know. You can't believe what they did!

This is how I feel when I read the story of how Judas makes the decision to betray Jesus. I want to know how he could ever possibly think of betraying Jesus…the One whom he loves and the One whom he has followed over the past three years and learned so much from. Why in the world would he do something like this?

Let's recap what's going on here: Jesus has entered into Jerusalem (remember, He came in riding on a donkey and people praised Him). Jesus and His disciples came to Jerusalem because it was time for the Passover Festival (a Jewish festival that is celebrated to help them remember when God freed them from being slaves in Egypt). Jesus taught people, and most recently, He has cleared the temple of money changers (the people who charged large fees to exchange one's money for them in the temple).

The Bible tells us that Satan entered into Judas Iscariot and he made the decision to go talk to the chief priests. I'm sure he knew they did not like Jesus at all. So he decided he would help them out and look for a way to betray Jesus and give Him over to the chief priests and be arrested. What sweetened this decision for Judas is that they agreed to pay him.

Judas loved money and loved having a lot of it. He would get thirty pieces of silver for betraying Jesus. Thirty pieces of silver would be worth anywhere between $185-$216 in U.S. dollars today.[4] So Judas didn't make a whole lot of money for giving Jesus over to the chief priests and officials. It seems so crazy that Judas would do something like this for that much money. Was it worth it?

One thing we must learn from this story is how we need to forgive. Judas made a mistake…a HUGE mistake, and he knew it. We make mistakes every day, don't we? We must recognize those mistakes and ask God to forgive us and help us live better. He forgives you and He loves you. All He wants is for you to be close to Him.

Heavenly Father, forgive me when I mess up. Help me to make better choices and to listen to You. In Jesus' name, Amen.

---

4 https://en.wikipedia.org/wiki/Thirty_pieces_of_silver

Follow Me

Make a list of things you need to ask God to forgive you for. Pray and ask forgiveness. Then tear up the paper as a way for you to know that God has forgiven you.

The Last Supper
Luke 22:7-23

"This is my body given for you; do this in remembrance of me." Luke 22:19b

Let's think about some things you will never forget how to do… how to eat, how to drink, how to brush your teeth (I didn't say you wouldn't forget to brush your teeth, but how to brush your teeth), how to brush your hair, how to take a shower or bath, how to walk your dog, how to take out the trash, how to wash clothes, and how to ride a bike. Unless you lose your memory, I think you will always remember how to do these things.

Jesus wanted to show His disciples (and us) how we could always remember Him. He wanted there to be a way that we would never forget Him…a way that every time we did that thing we would think of Him. That way was demonstrated to the disciples the night they had their last meal with Jesus.

They were gathered together in an upper room of a home. A meal was set before them at a table. The twelve disciples and Jesus reclined at the table and enjoyed a meal. At this meal was bread and wine. As He gave each of them some bread and gave them wine to drink, He said, "Do this in remembrance of me." (Luke 22:19b). Jesus wanted His disciples to think about Him and remember Him every time they ate bread and drank wine. Those things symbolized His body and His blood. Jesus gave His life for us and He wants us to remember the sacrifice He made for us and to remember how much He loves us.

This remembrance meal today is known as Communion. Every church celebrates it differently, but there is always two things present at this: bread and juice (some churches may use wine). Some churches dip the bread in the juice and some churches drink from small communion cups. It doesn't matter how you do it, but when you do it Jesus asks us to remember Him.

When your church takes communion again, think about Jesus and how He loves you so much that He died on the cross for you so that you could live forever with Him in heaven. Remember the story of the Last Supper that He shared with His disciples. Remember Jesus.

Loving God, thank You for Jesus. Help me never to forget how to remember Jesus. Amen.

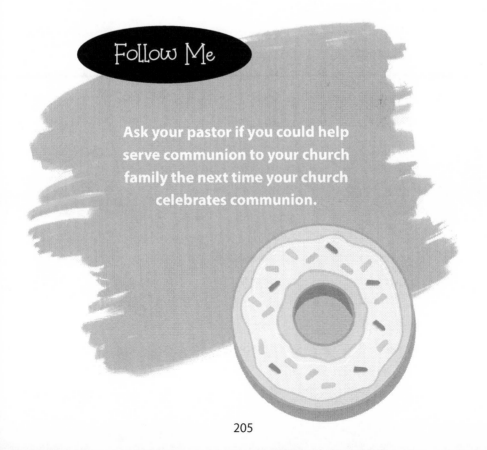

Follow Me

Ask your pastor if you could help serve communion to your church family the next time your church celebrates communion.

Garden of Gethsemane
Matthew 26:36-46

"Then he returned to his disciples and found them sleeping. 'Couldn't you men keep watch with me for one hour?' he asked Peter." Matthew 26:40

Have you ever been so sleepy that you just couldn't keep your eyes open? Maybe you needed to stay awake but for some reason your eyes kept shutting and you dozed off. It's hard to stay awake when you're super sleepy.

The disciples were feeling this same type of sleepiness the night they went to the Garden of Gethsemane with Jesus. It was nighttime. They had just had their last meal with Jesus so their bellies were full. Jesus wanted to go to the garden to pray. He asked the disciples to do one thing…stay awake and pray.

Jesus went off by Himself to pray (during this prayer time He became deeply saddened because He knew it was time for Him to give up His life). The disciples probably thought they could stay awake, but as they were sitting there their eyes just seemed to easily close. It was dark and they had full bellies. Sleep came easy for them.

When Jesus returned He found them sound asleep. He was a little upset because all He wanted them to do was pray while He was praying, too. Two more times He left them and came back to find them sleeping. Why couldn't they just stay awake?

How many of you can honestly say that you have fallen asleep while you have been praying? I will raise my hand and confess that I have! When you're lying in bed, tucked in and comfortable, and you're saying your prayers, you sometimes drift off in the middle of your prayer. The next thing you know you wake up and realize that you never finished praying! It's so hard to stay awake sometimes when you're praying, especially when it's nighttime. Your eyes are closed, you're praying in your mind and you can't help but fall asleep. You understand how the disciples felt that night!

My challenge to you is to work on staying awake while you pray! Keep your focus on God and praying to Him. Remember that Jesus wants you to stay awake and pray. He wants to talk with you. He wants you to talk to Him. And we must stay awake to do that!

Father God, You asked Your disciples to stay awake and pray. Help me do that and keep my focus on You. In Jesus' name, Amen.

Follow Me

Practice your prayer habits. If you pray at bedtime, sit up and keep your eyes open. Praying out loud helps you not only stay awake, but keeps your focus on Jesus.

Homemade Waffles

1 ¾ cup self-rising flour
½ cup oil
1 ¼ cup milk
2 eggs

Pre-heat waffle iron. Mix together flour, oil, and milk in a bowl. Separate the egg yolks from the egg whites and put them into different bowls. Beat the egg whites until fluffy. Add the egg yolks into the flour/oil/milk mixture and stir. After the egg whites are fluffy, stir them into the mixture as well. Pour into the waffle iron and bake.

Something To Chew On

· · · · · · · · · · · · · · · · · ·

What could you add into your daily
routine that would draw you closer
to Jesus?

One Way

John 14:1-7

"Jesus answered, 'I am the way and the truth and the life. No one comes to the Father except through me.'"
John 14:6

When you get old enough to drive, you're going to find out one thing…there are many different ways to get to a place. There are a lot of roads. Which ones are the quickest way to get to where you are going and which ones are the longest? Which ones are the straightest and which ones are more curvy? Which way is the best way?

In our passage today we learn something we all need to know… there's only one way to get to heaven to be with God. In this story we find Jesus talking to His disciples. He's talking about something that has the disciples confused. He keeps saying that He's going to leave and go to His Father's house (which has many rooms), and that He will come back for them and take them to be where He is. This makes no sense to the disciples and one of them (Thomas) speaks up and basically tells Jesus he doesn't understand what He's talking about.

Then Jesus says the words that we all need to hear: "I am the way and the truth and the life. No one comes to the Father except through me." (John 14:6).

I'm wondering if a light bulb went off in the disciples heads when He said this. Maybe not at that exact moment for them, but it can for us. Jesus tells us that the only way we can come to the Father is through Him. Jesus is the way…the only way.

In our world today there are some who will tell you that if you do good deeds and live your life right then that will get you into heaven. But we, as Christians, know that's not the way to get to heaven. Jesus tells us plain and simple that we must believe in Him because that's the ONLY way to God the Father who lives in heaven. In order for us to live forever with God we need to believe in God's Son, Jesus, as our Savior. We need to believe that He forgives us of our sins and that He came to this earth to save us.

Remember there is ONE way to heaven...and that is through Jesus Christ.

Heavenly Father, I want to live forever with You. I believe in your Son, Jesus, and what He did for me. Help me to share with others that Jesus is the only way to You. Amen.

Follow Me

Time to draw! On a sheet of paper, draw a cross at one end. Then draw a road leading up to that cross. And on the road write, "Jesus is the Way". Hang this in your room to remind you that Jesus is the only way to get to heaven.

The Holy Spirit

John 14:15-31

*"But the Advocate, the Holy Spirit, whom the Father
will send in my name, will teach you all things and will
remind you of everything I have said to you." John 14:26*

Ever heard of something called the Trinity? That's a way we refer to God. Here's something really hard to understand…God is three persons in one. We know God as the Father, the Son, and the Holy Spirit. God is our Father, the Son is Jesus Christ, and then there's the Holy Spirit. You may have heard of the Trinity, but you just aren't sure how in the world to understand it.

Let's take a look at our Bible verses today that might help you understand the Holy Spirit. Jesus is talking to the disciples about what is to come after He leaves this earth. I can just imagine what the disciples were thinking. They were confused, scared, shocked, unsure of what was going to happen. They might have even been thinking about how they were going to remember all that Jesus had taught them over the past three years. Jesus knew everything those disciples were thinking, too. He knew they would be worried. And that's when Jesus said that God promises to send the Holy Spirit. The Holy Spirit would be there to teach them and guide them and to help them remember everything He taught them. There was no need to fear and no need to worry.

Just as Jesus promised the Holy Spirit for the disciples, He promises it for us, too. When we believe in Jesus, we are marked with the seal of the Holy Spirit. The Holy Spirit will guide us in what we should do. The Holy Spirit will convict us of what we know we shouldn't do. The Holy Spirit will remind us of the teachings of Jesus and what we are to do. The Holy Spirit is alive and present in all those who believe.

I often tell my kids at church that the Holy Spirit is like the wind. You can't see it, but you can feel it and you can hear it. You know when the wind is moving because you can see the trees sway and you can feel the breeze on your body. You can hear it because of how it affects the trees all around you. Even if it's just the softest of breezes, you can still hear the faint whisper of it. And that's what the Holy Spirit is like for us. We can feel it, hear it, and see it moving. We just have to be open to it and listening for it.

So how do you know when the Spirit is talking to you or how can you feel the presence of the Holy Spirit? I like to explain this in a couple of ways. One way I can explain it is that I get chill bumps all over my body...even when it's not cold outside. It's like a breeze has blown over my body and I can just feel it. When I am sitting quietly spending time with God and truly being still, then I get those chill bumps and I know He is present and I can hear Him speaking. I also can feel the Spirit when I know I am supposed to do something. It's an overwhelming feeling where I know I am to act on something. Hard to explain except to tell you that you will just know when the Holy Spirit is talking.

Follow Me

Listen to the song "Holy Spirit" by Francesca Battestelli. This is my favorite song about the Holy Spirit. Let this be a time of worship with God.

I am so grateful that Jesus promised the Holy Spirit to His disciples and that He promises us the Holy Spirit today, too. Can you feel the Spirit? Can you hear the Spirit? I believe you can if you just take time to be still and listen.

Gracious God, thank You for the promise of sending the Holy Spirit to be with us on the earth after Jesus left. Help me to be still and listen for the Spirit. Amen.

Peace I Leave With You

John 14:27

"Peace I leave with you; my peace I give you. I do not give to you as the world gives. Do not let your hearts be troubled and do not be afraid." John 14:27

Do you ever get nervous when you have to take a test at school? Or do you get nervous before you play in your football or soccer game? I like to call them "butterflies in my stomach." They flutter around and keep me from feeling at peace. I don't like them. I like to feel peaceful at all times.

In our devotion yesterday, we heard Jesus promising the disciples that He would send the Holy Spirit to the earth once He was gone. I can probably guess that the disciples had some butterflies flying around in their stomachs, too. They didn't like to hear Jesus talk about a time when He would no longer be with them. It made them very nervous.

Maybe that's exactly why Jesus said what He did right after He promised to send the Holy Spirit. He knew what they needed to hear. "Peace I leave with you; my peace I give you. I do not give to you as the world gives. Do not let your hearts be troubled and do not be afraid." (John 14:27).

Jesus is telling them (and telling us) that we are not to be afraid of anything. Why? Because He is the One who will bring us peace. He gives it to us freely and offers it to us as a gift. But that peace is not the same type of peace the world offers to us. The world would say that we will have peace if we have a lot of money, nice clothes, big houses, and expensive cars. The world says we need stuff to make us happy. Jesus says we don't. We only need one thing, and that is Him.

Here's what you can do when you start to feel nervous or afraid. Close your eyes. Think of Jesus. And then think of a place you like to go that brings you peace. Maybe that's the beach, the river, your house, or outside in your yard. Then picture Jesus there with you. He's walking next to you or sitting beside you. He's there with you and His presence brings you overwhelming peace. I believe that when you can picture Jesus next to you, then you will have a peace that only Jesus can give.

Peaceful Lord, thank You for the reminder that You are the One who brings me peace. Remind me of Your presence with me when I am nervous or afraid. Thank You for being with me. Amen.

Follow Me

Next time you have a test at school or a big game to play, carry a cross in your pocket. This will help you be at peace and remind you that Jesus is with you. Then you can be calm and at peace and will rock that test or game!

Jesus is Arrested

Matthew 26:47–56

"Jesus replied, 'Do what you came for, friend.'"
Matthew 26:50

The time had come.

Jesus knew what was getting ready to happen to Him. He knew who was getting ready to betray Him. He knew that it was time to be arrested and stand trial and be crucified and die on the cross. He knew it all.

Jesus and the disciples were still talking in the Garden of Gethsemane when a large crowd of people came into the garden. They had swords and clubs like they were ready to fight. The crowd included chief priests and elders of the people. But then it also included a very familiar face…Judas Iscariot, one of Jesus' disciples. I can only imagine the look of shock that came over the disciples faces as they watched Judas enter into the garden with the bad guys. And then when they witnessed him kiss Jesus on the cheek and betray Him, they had to be so upset!

But none of this surprised Jesus. He wasn't shocked by Judas' betrayal. He didn't even fight when they arrested Him. He knew Judas was going to betray Him. He even told him in the garden to do what he came to do. He was ready to die.

The disciples, however, weren't so easy going with all this. They were extremely upset. Peter even got so mad that he grabbed a soldier's sword and cut off the ear of one of them! But Jesus quickly reprimanded Peter and healed the man by putting his ear back on.

They were ready and willing to stand up for Jesus—to do anything to protect Him.

What about you? Are you willing to stand up for Jesus? What would you do if all your friends didn't believe in Jesus and made fun of you for believing in Him? Would you follow the crowd and go along with their beliefs? Or would you be willing to stand up and say aloud that you believe in Jesus?

It's hard to go against what the whole crowd is doing, but we, as Christians, must be ready to stand up for Jesus. We must be willing to let others know that He loves them and cares for them…that He died for them so they could live forever. If we don't stand up…who will?

Father God, help me to always stand up for You and not be afraid to tell others about You. Give me courage and strength to share about You with others. In Jesus' name, Amen.

Follow Me

If given an opportunity in your writing or English/Language Arts class, write about why you love Jesus or why you are thankful for Him.

Peter Denies Jesus
Matthew 26:69-75

*"Immediately a rooster crowed. Then Peter remembered
the word Jesus had spoken: 'Before the rooster crows,
you will disown me three times.' And he went outside
and wept bitterly." Matthew 26:74b-75*

Think about who your best friend is. Now imagine they got ac-
cused of doing something they really didn't do. You really wanted
to support them, but at the same time you just wanted to stay out
of it and not associate with them. When others see you they question you saying, "Aren't you their best friend?" You quickly deny it
because you don't want to get in trouble, too.

But then you hear a sound that reminds you of your best friend
and all the fun times you have together. You remember why you
are best friends and you are ashamed that you have not supported
them more. You can't believe you would ever deny them being your
best friend just because you were afraid. And because of how guilty
and shameful you feel, you cried.

This same thing happened to Peter, one of Jesus' disciples. Some
like to say Peter was Jesus' best friend. Jesus told the disciples a lot
of things about what would happen soon to Him. But with Peter,
things were different. Peter and Jesus were pretty close friends.
However, Jesus told Peter something Peter believed would never
happen. Jesus said that when he heard the sound of a rooster crowing, Peter would have denied knowing Him three times. When Jesus
said that, Peter quickly said that would never happen. Why would
he ever deny knowing Jesus?

After Jesus was arrested and taken away, Peter followed Him, but
from a distance. He was afraid of getting too close because he might

be arrested, too. But Peter couldn't stay hidden. People were recognizing him as being one of Jesus' followers. Three different people questioned him and said he was one of the followers of Jesus. Each time he got angry and quickly denied knowing Jesus. Then he heard the sound of a rooster crowing and he instantly remembered what Jesus had said. How could he have done this? He was so ashamed that the Bible says he "went outside and wept bitterly." (Matthew 26:75b).

Peter did something you think you would never do. How could anyone who loves Jesus so much deny knowing Him? There may be a time in your life that this happens. I pray it never does. I pray you will cling tight to Jesus even in the hardest of times. I pray you will shout from the rooftops how much you love Jesus. I pray you will let your life shine the light of Jesus so brightly.

Will it be easy? Not at all. But remember Jesus loves you and we should always be willing to share Him with others.

Loving God, thank You for Jesus. Help me to work hard every day at showing His love to other people and to never deny knowing Him. I love You, Lord. Amen.

Follow Me

Give your best friend a small gift today. This could be a note telling them how much they mean to you or maybe even something yummy like a piece of candy. Let them know you are glad they are your best friend.

Crucifixion of Jesus
Matthew 27:32-56

"When the centurion and those with him who were
guarding Jesus saw the earthquake and all that had happened, they were terrified, and exclaimed, 'Surely he was
the Son of God!'" Matthew 27:54

The story of the death of Jesus is so very sad. I don't like talking about it because it always makes me cry. But it's what our life as Christians is centered on. If Jesus didn't die, what would our lives be like? So it's important to talk about Jesus' death even if it brings tears to our eyes and makes us sad.

Did Jesus deserve to die on the cross? Absolutely not! He had done nothing wrong. All He did was share about God, perform miracles, heal people, and love people. Nothing wrong about that. But we know how this story goes. Jesus is arrested and He's put to death by crucifixion...that's where a person is nailed to a cross and hung on there to die.

While Jesus was hanging on the cross, several things took place. First, His clothes were divided up and soldiers cast lots for them. They placed a sign over Him that said, "THIS IS JESUS, THE KING OF THE JEWS." (Matthew 27:37). They mocked Him and said really bad things about Him. The soldiers thought that if He was really God's Son then He could save Himself and He wouldn't die.

During that time, Jesus didn't speak much but He did utter something that's recorded in the Bible. He asked God a question. He wanted to know why God had abandoned Him. I believe it was in this moment that He was very much human and felt alone.

Then Jesus breathed His last breath and died. At that moment the earth shook and the rocks split open. And then something else amazing happened. The curtain in the temple was torn in two. You may be wondering what's so special about a curtain tearing, but here's why it matters: inside the temple there was a curtain that separated the Holy of Holies from everything else. The Holy of Holies was where the Ark of the Covenant was kept. This was where the presence of God was and no one could enter the Holy of Holies except the priest and only he was able to enter that sacred space once a year. That curtain represented our separation from God.

But now that the curtain was torn in two, it meant we were no longer separated from God. Jesus was the One who broke that separation because He took on all our sins and died for us so we could live forever in heaven. Does that make sense? Maybe it's hard for you to understand now, but I believe as you get older it will make sense to you.

Follow Me

Cut a cross out of construction paper. On it write "Jesus died so I may live." Put this cross in a place where you will see it every day. This will be a great reminder for you of the sacrifice Jesus made for you and will remind you of His love for you.

Jesus' death is sad. Sometimes we just want to skip over the crucifixion and death part and focus on His resurrection. But His death was what gave us free access to God. It is what we base our Christianity on. And it's a vital part of who we are as Christians. So let's thank God for sending Jesus to die for us. Without His death we would not be able to live forever with Him in heaven. And for that I am eternally grateful.

Loving God, I don't like to think about Jesus dying, but I am thankful that He gave His life for me. Help me to always remember You love me. In Jesus' name, Amen.

French Toast

4 large eggs
1 cup milk
2 tsp. vanilla extract
8 slices of bread (I like to use the thick Texas Toast slices)

In a bowl, combine eggs, milk, and vanilla extract until beaten together well. Dip both sides of bread into the mixture, coating them well.

Melt a little butter in an electric skillet or griddle. Then place coated slices of bread into pan. Cook until both sides are golden brown. Serve with powdered sugar or cinnamon (if you like) and lots of syrup!

Something To Chew On

· · · · · · · · · · · · · · · · ·

**How has God blessed your life with
sweetness this week?**

Jesus' Burial

Luke 23:50-56

"Going to Pilate, he asked for Jesus' body. Then he took it down, wrapped it in linen cloth and placed it in a tomb cut in the rock, one in which no one had yet been laid."
Luke 23:52-53

You are probably very familiar with the story of Jesus' death and the story of His coming back to life (His resurrection). But how familiar are you with what happened to His body after He died? Do you know where He was buried, and who took care of all that?

Joseph of Arimathea. Ever heard that name? That's the man who decided he wanted to take the body of Jesus and bury it. Joseph was a Pharisee from a town called Arimathea, which was about eight miles north of Jerusalem. The Pharisees were the religious leaders in Israel--the very ones who did not like Jesus, who got Him arrested and then crucified Him. So why was one of them willing to bury Jesus' body?

Joseph, however, was not like the other Pharisees. He actually believed in Jesus. He believed that Jesus was God's Son and that He was the Messiah, the One sent into the world to save us from our sins. The Bible tells us that Joseph was "a good and upright man, who had not consented to their decision and action." (Luke 23:50-51). He did not agree with the Pharisees and was very much against their plan to kill Jesus. Basically, Joseph was one of the good guys.

So he asked Pilate for the body of Jesus, and then took it and put His body in one of his tombs. He wrapped it in linen cloth and placed it in the tomb. He loved Jesus and wanted to do this one thing for Him.

I think this story of Joseph should remind us of something. We can't judge all people by how some of them act. Even though Joseph was a Pharisee, we know he didn't believe like them and he didn't act like them. We thought all Pharisees were bad, but we have learned that we were wrong about that. We call this "stereotyping" people. We see the way some people act and then we think all those types of people act the same way…which is not always true.

Try your best not to judge someone because of who they are associated with. Get to know a person and find out who they truly are. I believe you will be glad you did.

Holy God, thank You for Joseph of Arimathea. Thank You for helping me see that I am not to judge others. Help me to love as You love. In Jesus' name, Amen.

Follow Me

Talk with someone today that you normally don't talk to. Get to know them. Remember to love as Jesus loved.

He is Risen

Luke 24:1-12

"Why do you look for the living among the dead? He is
not here; he has risen!" Luke 24:5b-6

"He is risen! He is risen! He is risen!"

I can just hear the excitement in the women's voices as they screamed this to the disciples early that morning after they discovered the tomb was empty. The angels that appeared to them said they were looking in the wrong place for somebody that was alive. They were a little confused until the angels explained something to them. We find this in verses 6-8:

"He is not here; he has risen! Remember how he told you, while he was still with you in Galilee: 'The Son of Man must be delivered over to the hands of sinners, be crucified and on the third day be raised again.' Then they remembered his words." (Luke 24:6-8).

Jesus had told all His followers, including the women, that He would die and be raised to life again. Maybe no one really understood what He meant by that so they just forgot about it. They didn't think anymore about Him coming back from the dead. They threw that important piece of information out of their memories. That is, until the angels helped them remember. I love how all of a sudden the memories come flooding back and they remembered all that Jesus had told them about His death and resurrection. And they got so excited about what they remembered that they rushed to tell the disciples.

Do you sometimes forget things that you read and learn about Jesus and God that is found in the Bible? I know there are times when I read a verse and think to myself, *Why have I forgotten this even though I've read it before? How could I forget such a cool story like this from the Bible?*

But the reality is that we are just like the disciples and the women in the Bible. We sometimes forget things Jesus tells us through His Word. And that's okay. I am so grateful Jesus continually reminds us of what He says through what we read in the Bible, through our parents and grandparents, through our friends, through our pastor and teachers at church, even through songs we hear on the radio or in books we read. Jesus is always speaking to us. Let's try hard to remember what He says to us each day.

Loving God, thank You for reminding me all the time about You. Help me to work hard at remembering what You say to me. In Jesus' name, Amen.

Follow Me

A great way to remember what Jesus says to you is to write it down. If you're reading the Bible, highlight what stands out to you and then write it down in a journal. If you hear a song and the words speak to you, write it down. If you like something your teacher or pastor says to you at church, write it down. We can remember things better if we write them down.

Jesus Appears to Mary Magdalene

John 20:11-18

"He asked her, 'Woman, why are you crying? Who is it you are looking for?'" John 20:15

Mary Magdalene is extremely upset. She had come to the tomb of Jesus to anoint His body with spices. But when she arrived, she found the stone rolled away and the tomb empty. In this chapter of John, we find Mary Magdalene outside the tomb crying. Imagine that you were Mary Magdalene and you couldn't find the body of Jesus. I have a feeling you would have been outside the tomb weeping as well.

But then she decides to peek her head inside the tomb and she finds two angels dressed in white. They ask her why she is crying, and she tells them it's because the body of Jesus is missing. Then she turns around to find a man standing by her. He asks her the same thing, "Woman, why are you crying? Who is it you are looking for?" (John 20:15). She doesn't know the man because we read that it says she thinks he is a gardener, someone who helps take care of the tombs.

But then this man says her name, "Mary." Upon hearing her name spoken, her eyes are opened and she recognizes this man. It is Jesus! He is alive!

There are two things I love about this story. First is that Mary Magdalene was the very first person Jesus appeared to after His resurrection. He didn't appear to His disciples first. He came to Mary Magdalene, a woman who loved Jesus and was a devoted follower of His. The second thing I love is how Mary Magdalene recognized Jesus after He said her name. When He gently said her name she knew it was Jesus. Her eyes were opened to see that Jesus really was alive. And she saw Him--all because He called her name.

Jesus is calling your name, too. Do you hear it? He may not scream it or yell it. He may just whisper it. That's why it's important for us to take time to be still (something I know that's hard to do as a kid). But Jesus is calling your name. He wants you to follow Him. He wants you to tell others about Him. Can you hear Him? He is calling…

Father God, help me to take time to slow down and listen to You. Thank You for calling me to follow You. Help me to obey and follow You at all times. In Jesus' name, Amen.

Follow Me

One way to help encourage people is to say their name. I know it may sound silly, but think about it…don't you like it when people know your name and call you by your name? When you pass someone in the hall say hello to them and say their name. For example, "Hey Annie!" I am sure you will see a big smile come across their face.

The Road to Emmaus

Luke 24:13-35

"When he was at the table with them, he took bread,
gave thanks, broke it and began to give it to them. Then
their eyes were opened and they recognized him, and he
disappeared from their sight." Luke 24:30-31

One day, two followers of Jesus were walking on the road to Emmaus, a village that was about seven miles from Jerusalem. They were busy discussing all the events that had taken place over the past few days, from Jesus' arrest and death to His resurrection. Suddenly Jesus came up to them and walked with them. But do you think they recognized Him as Jesus? No, they did not. He kept them from recognizing Him for the time being. I'm not sure what His reason was. Maybe He wasn't ready to reveal Himself just yet.

It's hard to imagine they didn't even recognize Him. How can they not realize it was Jesus, their friend, the one whom they had been learning from and following for the past three years? How did they not recognize His voice or figure out who He really was in the time He spoke to them? It's hard to believe.

But the thing Jesus did to open their eyes was that He broke bread, gave thanks for it, and gave it to them. After this happened, their eyes were opened, and they saw Jesus.

Are your eyes open to see Jesus today? I'm not talking about seeing Jesus' physical body, but we can see Jesus everyday if we just open our eyes and look. Jesus is in other people, in creation, and in every single thing. We just need to have our eyes open and look for Him. Do you see Him?

Creator God, thank You for my eyes. Help me to use them to see Jesus in my world today. Amen.

Follow Me

Take time today to open your eyes and actually look at everything around you. Write down what you see at different times throughout the day. At the end of the day, go back and thank God for all the things you saw.

Jesus Appears to the Disciples

Luke 24:36-49

"Then he opened their minds so they could understand the Scriptures." Luke 24:45

The twelve disciples still had not seen the risen Jesus. They had heard from the women that His body was not in the tomb. They ran to the tomb to see for themselves. But they had yet to see Jesus alive. Mary Magdalene had seen Jesus, and two other friends had seen Jesus on the road to Emmaus, but not them. When would Jesus show Himself to His close friends?

In the moment when they were discussing Jesus appearing to their two friends on the road to Emmaus, Jesus appeared to them! They were in such a state of shock, I think, because Jesus said it looked like they had seen a ghost. He even showed them His hands and feet and let them see the scars. And He also told them to touch Him so they would realize He was real.

Then Jesus goes on to say how everything that happened to Him had to happen so the Scripture could be fulfilled. And then I love what He does next, "Then he opened their minds so they could understand the Scriptures." (Luke 24:45).

You see, the disciples still didn't believe it all. Like I said, I think they were in shock, but also overjoyed that their friend, their Savior, was alive. Still, they didn't quite understand everything. So Jesus opened their minds and they were able to finally understand what had taken place and why. I can just picture the disciples faces as they understood what Jesus said. Like a light bulb had gone off and it all made sense!

Have you ever read Scripture and just didn't get it? I know there are times when I don't understand it either. I read it over and over and it just doesn't make sense. But I found something that helps me understand the Bible – I pray before I read the Bible. I ask God to give me wisdom to understand what I'm reading so I can see and hear what God is speaking to me. And you know what…when I do that, I actually find it easier to understand!

So when you get frustrated because you don't understand… pray. And then read and watch God set off that light bulb in your mind!

Almighty Father, I want to understand Your Word. Give me wisdom as I read the Scriptures and help me understand what You are speaking to me. In Jesus' name, Amen.

Follow Me

Did you read something in your Bible that made sense and you understood it? If so, share it with your parents. When you share it, then you will be helping other people understand God's Word, too.

Doubting Thomas

John 20:24-29

"Then he said to Thomas, 'Put your finger here; see my hands. Reach out your hand and put it into my side. Stop doubting and believe.'" John 20:27

Has anyone ever told you something that seemed really hard to believe? Like the story they shared with you just seemed so outrageous there was no way what they said could have happened. It seemed impossible.

That is exactly how Thomas, one of Jesus' disciples, felt the day the other disciples told him that Jesus was alive. Poor Thomas was not in the house where the other disciples were when Jesus appeared to them. The Bible doesn't tell us where Thomas was, just that he wasn't with the others. He missed out on the first appearance of Jesus to the disciples.

But you would think that when the disciples came and told Thomas about what happened that he would believe, right? Thomas had been with Jesus for the last three years and he had seen all the miracles Jesus had performed. He knew Jesus could do miraculous things and he knew his friends would never lie to him, right? But for some reason Thomas said he would not believe that Jesus had risen from the dead until he could put his finger where the nails had been and put his finger in Jesus' side. He had to see it for himself to know that it was true. He wasn't taking the word of his friends on this one.

About a week later Thomas finally gets his wish. Jesus appears again to all the disciples (and Thomas too). Jesus tells Thomas that he can put his finger where the nails have been and in His side. And then Jesus says to Thomas, "Stop doubting and believe." (John 20:27b). (On a side note…that's why you might hear others call him "Doubting Thomas.")

Maybe there have been times in your life when you have doubted Jesus. Maybe you didn't believe He would provide for your family when you needed help. Maybe you didn't believe He hears your every prayer. Maybe you didn't believe He loves you because you have done some bad things. Maybe you have been a doubter…just like Thomas.

Follow Me

Write the word "BELIEVE" on a sheet of paper. Tape it where you will see it everyday. Let it be a reminder for you to believe in Jesus at all times.

I pray you will take your doubt to God and ask for forgiveness. And then believe. Trust in Jesus with all your heart. Know He will provide. Know He hears your prayers. Know He loves you no matter what.

Faithful God, thank You for loving me. Help me to always believe in You and trust in You even if it seems impossible. In Jesus' name, Amen.

Spiced Tea

20 oz. jar of Tang
20 oz. jar of Lemonade powder
½ cup instant tea
2 tsp. cinnamon
1 tsp. cloves
1 tsp. nutmeg

Mix all ingredients together. Put 3-4 spoonfuls of spiced tea in a teacup. Boil water in a teapot. Once it boils, add water to the teacup. Mix well and serve hot.

Something To Chew On

What topic of conversation would you strike up with Jesus while enjoying a cup of tea together?

Breakfast on the Beach
John 21:1-14

"Jesus said to them, 'Come and have breakfast.'"
John 21:12

If you could pick one person to have breakfast with, who would you pick?

Some of you might say your favorite cartoon character, a favorite actor or actress, a character from a video game, a favorite athlete, a favorite author, a favorite musician or singer, or maybe even the President of the USA.

But what if you could have breakfast with Jesus? Like really have breakfast with Him -- you could physically see Him with your eyes and know that He was present with you. What would your reaction be? Would you be in awe? Would you be in shock? Would you be nervous or scared? Would you talk a lot or hardly any at all? Would you even know what to say to Him? What would you do if Jesus said to you, "Come and have breakfast?"

The disciples got to experience this early one morning after they had seen Jesus alive. They were out fishing and hadn't caught much. Then a man on the shore told them where to drop their nets and when they did, they caught 153 fish! It was then they recognized that man to be Jesus. Peter was so excited, he jumped off the boat and swam to shore (even though the boat wasn't far from shore). He was just excited to see Jesus!

Then Jesus invited them to come and eat breakfast with Him. And guess what they ate? Fish! (I can't say I've ever had fish for breakfast before!) I believe the disciples were thrilled to see Jesus once again (this was the third time He had appeared to them after His resurrection). I believe they talked a lot to Jesus early that morning at breakfast. I believe they wanted to soak up as much of Jesus as they could and were eager to talk and listen to Him.

Jesus not only invited the disciples to eat breakfast, but He invites us to eat breakfast with Him, too. I pray this devotional book has helped you open your Bible and spend time with Him. I pray you get as excited as Peter when he was on the boat about spending time with Jesus. Will you accept the invitation from Jesus to have breakfast with Him every morning? I know He is waiting to spend time with you.

Holy God, thank You for inviting me to have breakfast with Jesus. Help me to always be excited about spending time with You. In Jesus' name, Amen.

Follow Me

Invite a friend or neighbor over for breakfast today. Make them breakfast using one of the recipes in this book.

Peter, Do You Love Me?

John 21:15-19

"When they had finished eating, Jesus said to Simon Peter, 'Simon son of John, do you love me more than these?' 'Yes, Lord,' he said, 'you know that I love you.' Jesus said, 'Feed my lambs.'" John 21:15

Have you ever gotten frustrated with someone because they kept asking you the same question over and over again? You were okay with them asking you a second time, but it got annoying after the third and fourth times and you gave the same answer each time. You might have even been to the point where you were about to blow your top! Why do they keep asking you the same question?

You might say Peter felt frustrated that morning on the beach after he had finished breakfast with Jesus. Jesus kept asking Peter if he loved Him. Why would He keep asking a silly question like that? Of course Peter loved Jesus. After the third time, Peter began to feel hurt. Surely Jesus knew that Peter did love Him very much!

Jesus' response after Peter said "yes" all those times when He asked him if he loved Him, was a simple reminder to "Feed my lambs. Take care of my sheep. Feed my sheep." (John 21:15b, 16b, 17b). Was Jesus really asking him to take care and feed His sheep that lived in the pasture? No. The sheep Jesus was referring to were people like us. All of us are considered sheep and Jesus is our Shepherd (remember our devotion on the Good Shepherd?).

Jesus is making sure Peter realizes the importance of taking care of all the people. He wants Peter to know that his call is to go out and let others know about Him and to preach His Word to everyone.

Fill in the blank with your name and answer this question. Remember this call is not only for Peter, but for you, too.

_____, do you love me? Yes, Lord, you know that I love you.

If you love me, _____, take care of my sheep.

Father of All Things, I love You so much. Help me to always take care of others and let others know about You. Amen.

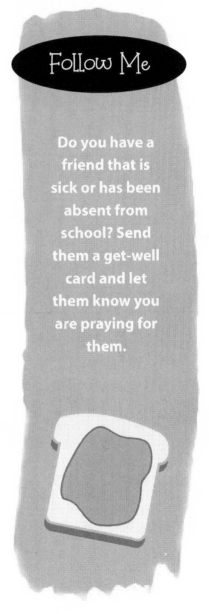

Follow Me

Do you have a friend that is sick or has been absent from school? Send them a get-well card and let them know you are praying for them.

Jesus' Ascension

Luke 24:50-52 & Acts 1:1-11

"While he was blessing them, he left them and was taken up into heaven." Luke 24:51

How many of you like to wait?

We live in a world today where we can get pretty much anything we want right when we want it, right? The internet has allowed us access to so many things instantly. So when it comes time for you to wait for something, I am thinking you may have a hard time with it.

In this Bible story today, we find Jesus telling the disciples they will have to wait for the arrival of the Holy Spirit. Remember…Jesus had risen from the dead and He had appeared to His disciples and other people over the course of forty days. At the end of this time, He called His disciples together to a place called the Mount of Olives, which was outside Jerusalem. He blessed them. And He gave them a simple command…wait. He said, "Do not leave Jerusalem, but wait for the gift my Father promised, which you have heard me speak about. For John baptized with water, but in a few days you will be baptized with the Holy Spirit." (Acts 1:4).

After He said that, He was taken up in a cloud and they could see Him no more. This is what we call the Ascension of Jesus. He went up to heaven to be with God. When this happened, they were not sad like they were when He died. They knew they would see Him again one day. All they had to do now was wait. Jesus promised He would send the Holy Spirit to give them power to witness, which means to go out and tell others about Jesus and who He is. It's what we call the way we share our faith and lead others to come to know Jesus as their Savior, too.

So the disciples had to wait ten days. That doesn't seem like a long time, but when you are ready to get something, then it seems like forever!

I believe the disciples were ready for the Holy Spirit, but I don't believe they whined or complained about how long it was taking (something we tend to do).

I love what the Bible says they did while they waited: "They all joined together constantly in prayer, along with the women and Mary the mother of Jesus, and with his brothers." (Acts 1:14). Isn't that so awesome? They prayed! And I believe they waited patiently for the arrival of the Holy Spirit. Ten days probably passed by fast because they prayed and waited patiently. And when the Holy Spirit did come, it was so worth the wait!

Sometimes when we pray, we think God will answer our prayer instantly, right? But we need to realize He doesn't always do that. Can He answer instantly? Absolutely. But sometimes He makes us wait…just like the disciples had to wait for the arrival of the Holy Spirit.

What I want you to do while you wait is to pray. Ask God for patience in helping you wait. Let's practice being good waiters and praying while we do so.

Dear God, thank You for always giving us what You promised. Thank You for the Holy Spirit. Help me to be patient while I wait for You to answer my prayers. Help me to remember that You hear me and that You love me, In Jesus' name, Amen.

Follow Me

Let's unplug today! Make it a phone-free, tablet-free, computer-free day. No internet, no video games, no phone games or tablet games. Unplug from your electronics today and enjoy having to wait!

Many More

John 20:30-31 & John 21:25

"But these are written that you may believe that Jesus is the Messiah, the Son of God, and that by believing you may have life in his name." John 20:31

We have spent the past one hundred days diving into the life of Jesus. We have gone all the way from Jesus' birth to His death to His resurrection and to His ascension. We have read stories that are found in the Gospels (the first four books of the New Testament) that detail what Jesus' life was like while He was on this earth. We have learned things He did…which are pretty amazing, right? He has healed people, showed compassion to others, preached about God, taught people about God, ate dinner with sinners, brought people back from the dead, shown kindness to others, and most importantly, He loved others unconditionally.

In two different chapters at the end of the book of John (John 20 & John 21), we read something John writes that is eye opening. I am thinking that maybe you think we know everything there is to know about Jesus, right? I mean…there are four books of the Bible dedicated to teaching us about who Jesus was and what Jesus did. I bet you are thinking there is no way in the world there could be anything else we don't know about Him.

John says: "Jesus performed many other signs in the presence of his disciples, which are not recorded in this book. But these are written that you may believe that Jesus is the Messiah, the Son of God, and that by believing you may have life in his name." (John 20:30-31).

Oh wow! We are just scratching the surface in these first books of the New Testament. We don't know every single story there is to know about Jesus. He performed so many other signs that aren't even written down in one of these four books (Matthew, Mark, Luke, John). But the stories that we do know are written in this book for you and for me. They are written so that we might believe in Jesus as the Messiah, our Savior. Did you get that? They are written so YOU might BELIEVE in Jesus. Pretty awesome, right?

The very last verse in the book of John says that if every story about Jesus was written down there would not be enough room in the whole world for all the books. John lets us know that Jesus did so much more than could ever be written down. I hope that gives you a little insight into seeing just how magnificent Jesus is.

I hope you have learned something new about Jesus over the past one hundred days and I hope you have grown closer to the Lord as you have spent time with Him. But just because our devotions have come to an end, I don't want you to stop spending time with Jesus. Wake up every day and have breakfast with Jesus. Open your Bible and read God's Word. Spend time in prayer. Get to know Jesus more and more each day. Draw closer to Jesus and live your life following Him.

Almighty God, thank You for giving me Your Word to read so I can learn more about You. Help me to spend time with You every day. And help me to be brave and share about You with others. In Jesus' name, Amen.

Follow Me

Start reading books in the Old Testament. My favorite is the book of Joshua. I love how God uses Joshua to help the Israelites move into the Promised Land. While you read, write down some of your favorite parts of each book.

About the Author

Vanessa Myers has a passion for teaching kids about Jesus and desires for each of them to spend time with Him daily. She is a graduate of Duke Divinity School and has been serving in the ministry since 2001. She is the Children's Ministry Director at Dahlonega United Methodist Church in Dahlonega, GA. She is also the author of Rise Up: Choosing Faith over Fear in Christian Ministry and Adventures: An Advent Devotional for Women. She is married to Andrew and they have two children. She enjoys sharing about her faith, family, and ministry on her blog: www.vanessamyers.org.

Made in the USA
Columbia, SC
16 January 2020